PRAISE FOR BYE-BYE BOARDROOM...

"If you plan to exchange your attaché case for a diaper bag, this book will help get you there. *Bye-Bye Boardroom; Confessions From A New Breed Of Stay-At-Home Moms* shows women how they can lead fulfilling lives as they raise their brood. The book represents what thousands of well-educated, ambitious women have experienced once they replaced million dollar mergers with muppetry and Gerber. You will laugh, you will cry, and we'll be there when you do."

—Christine Louise Hohlbaum
Stay-at-Home Mom, Paunzhausen, Germany

"The book is timely because women are finding that the pot of gold at the end of the corporate rainbow is not really worth very much compared to the time they spend away from their children while they are growing up. This book will show women that leaving a well paying job can be a good thing when done to accomplish certain important family and personal goals. Here's how other women have done it—you can too!"

—Donna Maria Coles Johnson
Stay-at-Home Mom, Bowie, Maryland

"The 'What to Expect' series of books can't touch this. These are the real-life stories and dramas of everyday parenting no one ever tells you about. If you're a new stay-at-home mom or planning on becoming one, you'll need to read this. And don't say we didn't warn you!"

—Christine Velez-Botthof
Stay-At-Home Mom, Birmingham, Alabama

"We've come a long way, baby, but the journey is far from over... Essential text for women exchanging fulltime corporate chaos for the ultimate challenge—full-time motherhood."

—Donna B. Jones
Stay-At-Home Mom, Altamonte Springs, Florida

"Trading in my leather briefcase for an SUV with a collapsible third row, giving up power lunches for a family pass to the zoo, packing up the zippy Ann Taylor coordinates for wash and wear cotton separates...Giving up my career to stay at home to raise my kids wasn't the end of my life...it was the beginning of it."

—Mary Susan Buhner
Stay-At-Home Mom, Fishers, Indiana

"With the accumulation of currency being our cultural measure of effort and output, the value of motherhood and its contributions to stable and well adjusted communities has been greatly diminished. This book is a great window into the minds of intelligent, driven women who decided that being Superwoman is not as important as just being MOM."

—Ieshia Ali
Stay-At-Home Mom, Bryn Mawr, Pennsylvania

"The transition from juggling conference calls, board meetings and corporate takeovers to balancing playgroups, scout meetings and PTA functions is all too common for moms today. Those of us with business cards that now read 'Stay-At-Home Mom' are fortunate enough to reap the benefits of the most rewarding job of all...raising children!"

—Lisa Spengler
Stay-At-Home Mom, Franklin, Tennessee

BYE-BYE BOARDROOM

Other Books in the Capital Ideas for Parents Series:

FATHER'S MILK: Nourishment and Wisdom for the First-Time Father by Andre Stein, Ph.D. with Peter Samu, MD

FROM HIGH HEELS TO BUNNY SLIPPERS: Surviving the Transition from Career to Home by Christine Conners, MA

GOLDEN RULES OF PARENTING: For Children & Parents of All Ages by Rita Boothby

A GRANDMOTHER'S GUIDE TO BABYSITTING: Times Have Changed Practical Advice and Space for Important Information by Ruth Meyer Brown

HOW TO AVOID THE MOMMY TRAP: A Roadmap for Sharing Parenting and Making It Work by Julie Shields

THE MAN WHO WOULD BE DAD by Hogan Hilling, founder of Proud Dads, Inc.

Save 25% when you order any of these and other fine Capital titles from our Web site: www.capital-books.com.

BYE-BYE BOARDROOM

Confessions from a New Breed of
Stay-At-Home Moms

Rachel Hamman

Capital Ideas for Parenting

CAPITAL
BOOKS, INC.
Sterling, Virginia

Capital Books, Inc.
P.O. Box 605
Herndon, Virginia 20172-0605

ISBN 10: 1-933102-17-9 (alk.paper)
ISBN 13: 978-1-933102-17-7

Library of Congress Cataloging-in-Publication Data

Hamman, Rachel.
    Bye-bye boardroom : confessions from a new breed of stay at home moms/Rachel Hamman.
        p. cm.
    Includes index.
    ISBN 1-933102-17-9 (pbk. : alk. paper)
    1. Stay-at-home mothers. 2. Work and family. 3. Choice (Psychology) 4. Parenting—Psychological aspects. 5. Life change events. I. Title.

    HQ759.46.H35 2006
    306.874'30922—dc22

                                                    2005032943

Printed in the United States of America on acid-free paper that meets the American National Standards Institute Z39-48 Standard.

First Edition

10 9 8 7 6 5 4 3 2 1

Dedicated to Brad,
for making me a Mom

ACKNOWLEDGMENTS

I'D LIKE TO THANK MY PUBLISHER, Kathleen Hughes. Without her help, the book would still be a diary! Equally important are the 28 women who agreed to share their personal stories about leaving the boardroom and becoming stay-at-home moms. The fact that they were open and willing to join this project is what made the experience so worthwhile for me. I also want to thank my friends and family who gave me endless encouragement (and also gave me so much to write about!). Lastly, I want to thank you, the reader, for choosing this book. I look forward to hearing from more women who have either already embarked on this journey or who are considering making the move to become a stay-at-home mom!

Please visit me at: www.RachelHamman.com

CONTENTS

FOREWORD

W HEN I MADE THE LEAP from corporate America to carpool America, I didn't know what I was in for. The seemingly simple move of trading in my briefcase for a diaper bag unearthed a mountain of emotions that I was not quite ready or equipped to deal with. As a formerly confident, organized, and effective leader, I found myself having to navigate in uncharted territory. I had negotiated big contracts, landed mammoth business deals, created corporations, and gone toe-to-toe with savvy CEOs, but nothing had prepared me for being a full-time stay-at-home mom.

The last year has been an incredible journey. Initially, I experienced a loss of identity, feelings of isolation, and pure dread. Throughout the transition, however, I realized that these feelings were extremely natural occurrences and that a multitude of women were finding themselves racked with guilt for not loving *every* minute of being home with their children. I emerged from the year with a renewed sense of self and an empowering way to redefine Women's Lib.

Bye-Bye Boardroom; Confessions From a New Breed of Stay-at-Home Moms is intended to be a comical, yet earnest look into the hearts and minds of women who have already made the transition out of the boardroom and others who are rushing back in. I extend a heartfelt thanks to the women who were willing to share their intimate stories about being a stay-at-home mom. When you open these pages, you are treated to a glimpse of each of their lives, coupled with a peek at their souls.

The book will certainly entertain you, but more importantly, I hope that the book will let you know that you are not alone!

PART I

RACHEL'S DIARY

CHAPTER 1

LEAVING CORPORATE AMERICA FOR CARPOOL AMERICA

I HAD AN AFFAIR. I've had a love affair with the notion of being in business ever since I was old enough to remember. The entrepreneurial spirit seized me at a young age. As I sat in the smoldering Florida heat, at the prepubescent age of nine, peddling my over-sugared lemonade from a roadside stand, I dreamt of a plush office, me sitting with stiletto-clad heels crossed atop my mahogany desk, confidently steering the course of my Fortune 500 company. I would be whisking away on exotic business trips, closing deals across the country, and carving out my destiny in corporate America. Hell, I not only wanted to climb the ladder of success, I wanted to add extra rungs to the ladder to make sure it was challenging enough.

Being the classic overachiever, with a dash of feminism thrown in, whatever I pursued, I did it with the fervor a starved bulldog has when attacking a juicy steak. I had made my mark in the male-dominated investment industry when I worked for an international investment and brokerage firm, which shall remain nameless (for logo, think large animal with horns and a giant testicle sac). After seven years, I was in a successful practice, managing over a quarter of a billion dollars. To the untrained eye, it looked as if I had it all—the finely appointed office, lavish trips, stature in the community, and financial freedom.

That is why it came as a shock to my investment colleagues and clients when I announced that I was leaving my practice to start a children's charity. Close friends and family were also dumbfounded. "How can you just pick up and leave a successful career and start from scratch? And more importantly, why would you do it for no pay at all?" they bellowed. I explained that the view from "the top" was financially rewarding, but something was missing. I wanted to create something worthwhile. I wanted to fill a need that wasn't being addressed. I wanted to leave a legacy in my community.

Hence, The Golden Rule Foundation was born. My brother and I abandoned our respective lucrative careers and went about planning and devising how we could reach the most children possible with our message. The mission of the charity is to teach children the importance of giving to others by providing them with the opportunity to do hands-on, community service projects of their choice.

The foundation grew rapidly, from one participating elementary school in 1999 to over 44 participating elementary schools just five short years later. We were having a profound impact on close to 4,000 children per year and enriching their lives, as well as the lives of all the beneficiaries of the projects they implement. Everything was going swimmingly. What a feeling of pride and gratification from seeing the vision we had turn into something real, something tangible.

That is why the Board of Directors for The Golden Rule Foundation was baffled when I announced that I was retiring. Shock and disbelief swept over the room like the plague.

"What do you mean retiring?" they clamored.

"Well, I am planning to leave to be a stay-at-home mom. The foundation is stable enough and has a solid enough following that we can safely transition to new management," I explained.

"This is a pivotal time for the charity! How could you think about leaving now?" one board member questioned incredulously.

"This is a pivotal time for my kids, Jessica who is thirteen years old and Zachary who is five, and it is time that I put my family first," I proclaimed.

It was almost an out-of-body experience. Who was this woman declaring her intentions to abandon the workplace? I was convinced that I had been beamed aboard the "Mother ship" and now, an alien pod had overtaken my body and was officially ending my career! But alas, it was I who had just drawn the proverbial line in the sand, taking my first steps out of the boardroom.

Family and friends had already started a lottery pool, taking bets on how long my so-called retirement would last. They knew my past all too well. During my maternity leave with my first child, Jessica, I grew restless after four weeks on leave. By the fifth week, I was making custom baby onesies and selling them to local boutiques.

Yet, undaunted by the naysayers' predictions, my excitement brimmed as I conjured up how I was going to spend my early retirement. At the age of 39, I had worked toward my business goals with unbridled passion, and I was planning to approach my newly acquired life in the same fashion. No longer desperate to dominate the business world, I wanted to focus on my personal goals. Topping the list was spending quality time with my children. It wasn't as if I didn't spend time with my children prior to now; it was just in short intervals between strategic business plans, marketing blitzes, and black-tie galas. Now, with the luxury of time, they would get a piece of the "real" me. Just one problem, and here's the catch...the "real" me didn't know how to function in the real world.

CHAPTER 2

EARLY DIARY ENTRIES

∾ Diary Entry 1 ∾

For my first official act in retirement, I was going to be a bum. I had worked for over two decades while seemingly never having taken a break. So, I figured that I had earned it. This meant staying in bed. This meant no shower. This meant eating Cheetos right out of the bag while watching the latest tearjerker on the Lifetime Movie Network.

Flash forward to six p.m.: My husband, Brad, who by the way is a saint, comes in after having picked up the kids.

"How was your day of leisure?" he asked while staring at my hair, which had taken on a life of its own.

"It was nice," I said dreamily.

Jessica asked me, "Are you sick?"

"No," I replied.

"Why did you stay in bed all day?" she questioned.

The joke about "why do dogs lick their balls?" flashed comically through my mind. The punch line being: "Because they can." I had already become a ball-licking dog.

∾ Diary Entry 2 ∾

I walked into my closet this morning and looked at my collection of Armani suits and Gucci pumps and figured that this is not appropriate "active wear" for the playground. My closet was now a clothes museum, where the works of art now hung, only to be admired but not touched. I did not own the obligatory Juicy Couture jogging suit that the "cool" moms in the carpool lane donned. Mental note to self: "Get clothes that don't have to be dry-cleaned, and Goodwill will be having themselves a banner week."

Went to the park with Zachary. We had a great time, but I sweated profusely while chasing him up and down the slides. Or, maybe just because my "mommy uniform," which was partly comprised of shorts two sizes too small, had caused the chafing between my legs to make fire.

∼ Diary Entry 3 ∼

Today, I went to Michael's, a local crafts store, to get an arsenal of crafts to make with the kids. I was determined that I was not going to be one of those mothers who plopped their kids down in front of the TV when they got home from school. We stocked the cart full with a myriad of different kits. We had a soap-making kit, a sand art kit, clay sculptures, and ceramic statues to paint.

"Can we do them today, Mommy?" Zach asked with large, puppy dog eyes.

"Sure we can!" I exclaimed.

I didn't realize until later that he meant do them *all*. So, what looked to me like a good two- to three-week supply of fun-filled afternoons boiled down to one big art extravaganza, culminating with some cherished works of art. Besides the actual crafts they made, I also had wax on my kitchen table, colored sand in my carpet, and paint on the walls. Well, it might not hurt to let them watch a little television.

∼ Diary Entry 4 ∼

Time for home improvements! The excuse of never having time to chase down contractors was all about to change. I whipped open the phone book and let my fingers do the walking.

"Hello, do you replace sod?"

"Yes, we have wallpaper that needs to be hung; how quickly can you get here?" "How much do you charge for steam cleaning carpets?"

An army of refurbishing masters had just been given the green light to descend upon our home. Now, this is progress.

∼ Diary Entry 5 ∼

The downside of my personal home improvement team was that you had to stay with them. Call me crazy, but although they are bonded, I just don't feel right about leaving strangers in my house. So, although I was getting my "honey-do" list whittled down, I had effectively just sentenced myself to being indoors for the foreseeable future. Was having a new bathroom fixture worth having to baby-sit a plumber in his mid 50s with more "crack" than an inner city neighborhood?

∼ Diary Entry 6 ∼

Since we were going to be relegated to staying indoors, I had a wild hair to get domestic. I have never been one to cook. When we built our house, the builder asked if we wanted double ovens, and I assured him that both would end up "virgins," and a microwave was the only vital thing. I confided in him that the kitchen was only for show, a mirage, if you will, that my children will pass and wonder, "What is this room for?"

So, I set out to the store, with a shopping list of all the ingredients I would need to prepare my culinary wonders for the upcoming week. Needless to say, I was out of my element. What the heck is cumin anyway?

After the trip to Publix, I swung by my local Williams-Sonoma. I have always revered their marketing genius, because for somebody who doesn't enjoy cooking, like an addiction, I am always compelled to buy a new gadget or cookbook when I'm in their store. I arrived home, confident in the knowledge that I had what it takes to transform my kitchen into something Julia Child would have been proud of.

Dinner was outstanding, if I do say so myself. Chicken Piccata, artistically fanned across angel hair pasta; freshly baked bread; an arugula salad with candied pecans and gorgonzola cheese; and for the grand finale, chocolate cake. My arteries were hardening just looking at it all. After Brad recovered from the shock that a full-course dinner had been prepared for him, we sat down and enjoyed the meal. Not too shabby, lady. Everyone cleaned his or her plate. After three hours of preparation, they better have.

◠ Diary Entry 7 ◡

Pest control people came. I wanted to make sure that now that I was cooking, nobody found a stray bug in their soup. Hence, the second day of the gastronomic explosion commenced. Penne pasta with cream sauce, garlic bread, Caesar salad, and tiramisu.

Today, I let the kids help with the preparation. This, however, extended the preparation time from three to four hours. So much for family bonding. Everyone left the table satisfied. The dog may also have been thrown a few scraps so that my feelings were spared.

◠ Diary Entry 8 ◡

It occurred to me that I might want to offset my 5,000-calorie meals with a workout once in a while. I had recently stopped going to my personal trainer, Grady, who for the past five years had successfully kept me from ballooning up. (Or, at least he made me feel guilty enough about my Krispy Kreme binges that I showed up at the gym twice a week.)

Although I was happy with the progress made in the health arena, my new lifestyle was all about togetherness. So, I went to the YMCA and signed up for a family membership. This way, while I took a class or hit the weights, I could bring the kids. Or better yet, while they were in school, I could do a barrage of classes and be in peak physical condition. I would have ab muscles that you could bounce a quarter off of.

I should have known by glancing at my YMCA photo ID badge that the face looking back at me had a cynical smirk. Did my subconscious self know that the card would not see the light of day too often?

◠ Diary Entry 9 ◡

Part of my new physical fitness regime was to start walking on a daily basis. The course I mapped out is a 1.8-mile walk around a serene lake in my neighborhood. I chose to walk at dawn so that I would be back in time to get the kids ready for school. So, out the door I went in my bright white (very Jerry Seinfeldesque) Nike sneakers. How practical, they not only provide extra spring but also have built-in reflectors so cars on the way to work don't plow me down.

As I rounded the first bend of the lake, it occurred to me that I have never had time alone. No time whatsoever had ever been just for me. Usually, even a bathroom break was filled with my dog and Zachary each clawing at the door, wanting my undivided attention. Thirty minutes without interruption! I'm convinced that the "runner's high" everyone speaks of is not adrenaline induced, but, instead, it is brought on by the sheer nirvana of being alone with oneself.

So, for the first ten minutes, I marveled at the revelation that I was by myself. For the second ten minutes, I grappled with what does one think about with this newly found alone time? The third ten minutes were occupied with mathematical calculations of how far I would have to walk to burn off tonight's dinner. Even *with* the new sneakers, Georgia is just too far.

∼ Diary Entry 10 ∼

Ha! And they said that I would not be able to last a week at home without going out of my mind. Well, the second half is purely debatable. I do admit I feel as though I am drowning in laundry. How in the world do four people generate so many dirty items? I always did laundry once a week before retirement ("BR"). Now, it seems as though I am joined at the hip to my fabric softener and dryer sheets. There was a slight (and I do repeat slight) feeling of accomplishment when the mounds of clothing "debris" were transformed into ready-to-wear, neatly folded pillars of clothing. Am I beginning to buy this shit?

It's drudgery.

∼ Diary Entry 11 ∼

The other coveted location that I visit, on an almost daily basis, is the grocery store. Maybe this is my connection with the outside world? As I roll my cart full of groceries down the air-conditioned aisles, I have the uncomfortable realization that I am in a state of flux. I am no longer part of the working class, but I have not yet transitioned to the stay-at-home clique. I have the distinct feeling that I am invisible. I feel as if I no longer matter. Okay, snap out of it.

"One pound of Boar's Head turkey, shaved please," I mumbled to the deli guy. As he smiled and rambled on about the weather, I became increasingly aggravated. Did he think that I didn't know about current events? Did he think that just because I wasn't in a business suit, I didn't have specific views on factors affecting our world? Did he think that just because I was dressed in sweats, I wasn't capable of discussing global warming or the war in Iraq?

More horrifying was the fact that I had been that deli guy. No, I never shaved meat for a living, but I was guilty of the preconceived notion that stay-at-home moms were all about Little League and PTA. God, I had unwittingly been a female bigot all these years and had never realized it.

What I now realized was that once one leaves the workforce, those around you seem to no longer view you as a center of influence or a source of information. Unless, that is, it has to do with a new recipe or a trick to get out grass stains from jeans.

I had not only given up my title, I had given up a part of my essence. I liked being sought out for advice. After all, I am a problem solver. I miss not being vocal. I miss the verbal jousting that occurs when you are trying to convince someone to see a topic from your point of view. Was I being ultrasensitive to my new surroundings, or was this reality? I could feel my brain cells diminishing as I rolled my cart out to my car, hearing the thoughts whirl in my head only slightly louder than the cart's wheels, which clicked incessantly.

∼ Diary Entry 12 ∼

Now that I was aware of this new dilemma of impending brain atrophy, I set out to do something about it. When I was working in the investment arena, my job necessitated that I read publications to keep abreast of industry changes. I read voraciously. My briefcase was always full with *The Wall Street Journal, Barron's,* or *Investor's Business Daily.* Likewise, when I ran The Golden Rule Foundation, I was reading *Philanthropy Today* and legislation briefs that could impact the non-profit world. So, in my off time, I would lose myself in pure fluff. I would read fashion magazines or trashy romance novels.

The tables had turned. I no longer needed an escape from the real world. What I did need, however, was something that would engage my mind. Gone were the copies of *Glamour* and *Vogue,* and in their place were issues of *Time* and *Newsweek.* My bedside bureau was now crammed with books like *The 911 Commission Report* and *The Art of War.* (Not exactly light reading.) Just because I departed from the business world, my mind did not have to completely disappear as well.

∼ Diary Entry 13 ∼

After close to two weeks of packing Jessica and Zach their respective school lunches, I think I had nearly perfected the skill. Since I no longer had the payoff of closing a big deal or orchestrating a media event, I could at least take pride in packing the best damn lunch for my kids that was humanly possible. No, my kids would no longer have to be subjected to unidentifiable cafeteria food. "Mystery Meat" and two-day-old mash potatoes used in Shepherd's Pie were no longer part of their routine.

I made each lunch with the appropriate balance of food groups. (This was from a woman who has spent her life convinced that carbohydrates were the only food group available!) How pitiful, I thought, that my newfound "thrill" and sense of self-worth came from packing their lunches. Now I understand the marketing slant of the "Choosy Moms Choose Jif" peanut butter campaign. Damn straight I was choosy. Selecting which peanut butter brand I used was about the only thing I *did* get to decide on during the day.

∼ Diary Entry 14 ∼

Several times today, I caught myself creating new ideas for a potential business. Without any conscious prompting, the ideas are flowing to me faster than a major league pitcher throws a ball. During the carpool run; while packing lunches; while folding laundry, my mind kept veering off task. I never thought that I was particularly good at multitasking, but apparently, when the first task doesn't take a great deal of mental prowess, there is a lot left over to work with.

I scolded myself and forced the ideas from my head. I *am* retired. I should be enjoying this "free time." Why can't I just sit back and enjoy myself like a normal person who has spent the last 20 years toiling in the trenches? My days just seem so monotonous and predictable.

I reluctantly shared some of the "hypothetical" business ideas with my family. Brad gloated because he had chosen two weeks as his entry into the "How long will Rachel really retire for?" pool. I reminded him that these are only business *ideas*. Retirement lasts until I actually implement them. "Just ideas," I repeated to myself, as if the repetition would lull me into a state of complacency.

∼ Diary Entry 15 ∼

I have been fighting the urge to shop. Shopping has always been my form of therapy. It's a primal instinct, similar to the "hunt and kill" instinct that the caveman possessed. There is nothing more satisfying than going out and coming back with bags brimming with shiny objects and things for our home. I've been suppressing this desire to shop so that I do not send Brad into cardiac arrest. I have consciously been scaling back my shopping addiction to just a few small items at a time. After all, I don't want to scare him into thinking he'll have to take on two extra careers just to support my habit. No, I'll keep my shopping in check. No big-ticket items, at least not right away.

∼ Diary Entry 16 ∼

The kids did not have school today, so I decided to take them to the beach. Even though the beach is about 45 minutes from Orlando, we don't go that frequently. I chalked this up to several reasons. Firstly, when I worked, it just wasn't worth it to me to spend an hour and a half in traveling time when we have a pool right in our backyard. Secondly, Zachary and Brad are so fair-skinned that after 15 minutes, their lily-white skin is the color of lobsters, and they are ready to go. Lastly, me in a bathing suit is something that is best left in private and not shared with complete strangers.

Well, I no longer had the time demands on my schedule, so excuse number one had disappeared. Excuses number two and three were overcome with sunblock 45 and me swallowing my pride. So, after we had packed a cooler filled with sandwiches and drinks and my BMW's trunk was filled with beach chairs, Nerf footballs, and Frisbees, we headed off to the coast.

With the beach almost in sight, my car began to gurgle and click. I immediately looked at my temperature gauge, and no sooner than I saw the needle well into the dangerous "red zone," my car lost all power. We coasted into a nearby Kentucky Fried Chicken and watched helplessly as smoke escaped from underneath my hood.

"Does this mean we can't go to the beach?" Zachary cried.

"This means something worse," I confirmed.

"What's worse than not making it to the beach?" he pleaded.

"Mommy thinks that her car just blew up! Believe me, it's worse," I tried to reason.

So, after AAA came to collect us and tow us back into Orlando, my mind began to spin. "Look at the bright side," I consoled myself. "You wanted to trade your car in anyway." Then my mind shuddered when I thought about what might be its replacement. I was not quite ready to turn over the keys to my sports car in order to get a "Soccer Mom" van.

∾ Diary Entry 17 ∾

After picking up my rental car, a huge white Buick that could double for a tank during times of war, I decided to drown my sorrows of my recent engine explosion by planning a dinner party. (This was the more economical choice for forgetting my troubles, due to the self-imposed shopping restriction I had in force.) Do I see a trend happening? I use food to calm my nerves. Emotional eating has saved me thousands in therapy but is also responsible for the clothes hanging in my closet, ranging from size 8 to size 12.

∾ Diary Entry 18 ∾

I have been driving my snazzy new ride, which makes me look like I should live in a condominium deep in the heart of Miami Beach. Losing my car was like losing the last connection that I had to my former life as an executive. All I would need now to make the transformation complete was to start collecting flamingo lawn ornaments for my yard.

I packed up Zachary for what seemed like the 12th birthday party this month. Brad and I usually switch off each week to do "Birthday Party Duty." An adult can only handle so many trips to Chuck E. Cheese's, the Science Center, and the bowling alley before sacrificing a part of his or her sanity.

Whatever happened to old-fashioned birthday parties? What's wrong with having a homemade cake coupled with "Pin the Tail on the Donkey?" Has our society become so jaded as to think that our children wouldn't appreciate the simple pleasures of celebrating their special day at home? Not my kids! Zachary is turning six in just a few short weeks and will get to experience the sheer joy found in the ancient ritual of a homespun birthday party.

∾ Diary Entry 19 ∾

Zachary decided on a pirate theme for his birthday. So, I went to Party City today and collected an assortment of swords, eye patches, and bandanas to transform his guests from six-year-old kids into swashbuckling mates.

When Jessica went through my bag of loot from the store, she looked at me in disbelief and said, "You *bought* invitations?"

"Yeah," I replied. "What about it?"

"Well," she continued, "you can make invitations that are *way* cuter than these."

In my previous life, the one where I didn't have a second to myself, I would have used the "no time" excuse card to back out graciously, but gone were those days. So, the next thing I knew, I was shamed into making 20 treasure maps (complete with burnt edges for authenticity's sake). Not only did they turn out looking good, but I got to play with matches to boot. Woohoo!

∾ Diary Entry 20 ∾

My five-course, homemade meals are catching up with me. I went to put on some dress pants to go meet a friend for lunch today, and there was no clearance over my hips.

Curse those stretchy play clothes. I was wearing sweatpants and T-shirts, and since I had not stepped on a scale in weeks, I had no clue until then that I had turned into Shamoo.

I would have to hang up my apron for the unforeseeable future...or at least until my pants zipped again.

~ Diary Entry 21 ~

Jessica is intent on getting into acting. My "Little Drama Queen" truly is a Drama Queen. She loves being on stage and in the limelight. Luckily for her, she has the talent to go along with the desire. (Unlike her passion for the violin a few years back...yikes.)

We selected her headshots today, and they were breathtaking. Literally, they took my breath away. My 13-year-old looked at least 17. Visions of "Pretty Baby" flew into my head. Not what the average mother wants for her child. Hey, maybe that's what my next calling will be. I can travel around to auditions with her and be a doting "Stage Mom" who lives vicariously through her daughter. So, I sent off her headshots to several would-be agents.

What I realized today was twofold: First, there isn't anything that I wouldn't do for my kids. Second, the envelopes at The Golden Rule Foundation's office tasted better than my supply at home.

~ Diary Entry 22 ~

In the name of helping a friend and simply wanting to get the hell out of Dodge, I convinced my buddy Melissa to try out for a reality show called "Project Runway." It's a show to highlight up-and-coming designers. At the end of the season, the designer left standing would have his or her collection featured during New York Fashion Week. Not too shabby! Not only does Melissa have talent, she is a quick-witted, sexy woman who would be perfectly cast for the "young mom" slot when they are seeking to typecast for the show.

"When is the tryout?" Melissa said, looking skeptical.

"Next week in Miami. Isn't that great? It's practically right in our backyard. It's destiny," I continued.

"Next week? I could never pull it together by then," she countered.

"Oh, please. You already have the clothes samples, and I will even go down there with you to keep you company," I replied.

So, the deal was sealed. Little did I know that this little adventure would turn into something straight out of the movie "Thelma & Louise." No, we did not hold up any convenience stores, carouse with strange men, or drive off any cliffs. We did, however, have to ditch Melissa's car and rent another at Enterprise due to an air-conditioning failure. Then, we had several near-death experiences driving on the roads of Miami Beach, culminating with running out of gas on the turnpike.

"How many times can one use AAA in a single weekend and not get canceled?" I asked with all honesty.

Melissa was not selected as a finalist, but she did make it through the first round. Apparently, the role of young, hip mom had already been cast in one of the five cities they had already visited. The experience, however, is one that neither of us would take back. It gave Melissa the confidence to know that her designs were taken seriously. It gave me anew the knowledge that on our next road trip, I would be doing the driving!

∼ Diary Entry 23 ∼

With the start of school comes the litany of forms they send home for parents to fill out. Usually, this task, although not a thrilling one, is done with ease. This year proved to be anything but easy. I breezed through the form all the way up to the point where they ask "Occupation of Mother." What was my occupation? In the past, "President" or "Executive Director" would grace the page. Now, I sat there having an internal debate as to what I should write. If I wrote "Retired," it sounded as if I was 65 years old, and I had been designated to raise my grandchildren. I just couldn't bear to write "Housewife" because that term just didn't seem to sum me up. The term "Housewife" conjured up images of me in a neatly pressed A-line dress accompanied with a starched white apron, while I fluffed my husband's pillows and fetched him his evening paper, slippers, and cigar.

I tried semantics: "Hmmmm, let me see about 'Stay-at-Home Mom.'"

Nope, I'm out more than in. "Domestic Manager." Pleeeease.

"Mother." Seems to fit, but again it looked obscure on the page.

After sitting in bed for 20 minutes, grappling with this quandary and covered in eraser shavings caused by my indecision, I finally settled on "Entrepreneur."

I was clearly having a hard time with this career switch. Why was it so hard to admit that I no longer was part of the corporate environment? Why was the title of "Mother" not fulfilling enough for me? Millions of women wear the title proudly and don't seem to have the need to apologize for the fact. Was I that shallow? Did I need to seek approval from others so badly that I let that dictate my actions?

If filling out a simple form had become this monumental stumbling block for me, I didn't even want to think how I would react during "Career Week" at Zach's elementary school.

∼ Diary Entry 24 ∼

I bought a sorbet/ice cream maker today for the kids. Okay, for *me* and the kids. I figured that it would be a nice old-fashioned activity we could all do together. Believe me, the activities that you can do with a 13-year-old and a six-year-old that will keep them *both* intrigued are few and far between.

Jessica actually was in charge of christening the machine. She decided to make raspberry sorbet. I was excited that our new hobby could also be well within the constraints of any diet that I would surely be on again in the near future. Fresh fruit, ice, and artificial sweetener seemed like a healthier alternative to my doughnut addiction. She presented me with a bowl of rich, berry goodness, which was both refreshing and sweet.

"Wow! This is wonderful!" I said, as Zach nodded in agreement. "I can't believe that it tastes so good with just the artificial sweetener and raspberries," I continued.

"What's artificial sweetener?" Jessica asked.

"The bottle that's on the baking shelf marked artificial sweetener," I retorted. "You didn't use real sugar did you?" I questioned, waiting for the answer that I knew was coming.

"Only about two cups," she answered innocently. So much for being able to zip those pants any time soon.

∿ Diary Entry 25 ∿

Jessica and I went down to Miami for a self-awareness seminar for teens. Although the course was meant to be thought-provoking for her, I think I was the one who needed the content more than she. Not only was I incapable of making an easy transition into this new role as "Super Mom," I was also rapidly approaching the big "4-0." An identity crisis coupled with a midlife crisis is not a pretty picture.

On the trip, my ego did, however, get a boost. We were on our way to dinner when a car full of college guys pulled up beside us. They began to flirt and motion for us to follow them. I flashed a smile and then pointed to my wedding ring. Jessica, of course, thought that it was extremely funny.

After I let my ego come down off its cloud, I was hit by several thoughts. First, I was thrilled that I could be mistaken for someone of college age. (Unless they had just finished watching "The Graduate," and they thought I could play the part of Mrs. Robinson.) Second, I was horrified that they thought my 13-year-old daughter looked old enough to be in college. Lastly, I had to find a happy medium in my wardrobe choices. I no longer wanted to dress like a corporate drone, but clearly, I did not want my new look to scream, "I want to seduce the pizza delivery boy!"

∿ Diary Entry 26 ∿

Back to hardcore shopping. I figured that three weeks was ample enough time to have waited, and besides, my credit card was burning a hole in my wallet. I reasoned that a few pieces of furniture, an appliance or two, and some new jewelry would actually soften the blow for Brad when I decided to buy a new car. It's all relative, right?

∿ Diary Entry 27 ∿

I know that I am hard up for some adult conversation. The phone rang today, and it was a campaign representative calling for one of the local officials running for office. Ordinarily, I would kindly but firmly explain, "I just don't have time right now" and get them off the line. This time, however, I began to ask questions of the volunteer.

I started firing questions left and right. "With what party is he affiliated?"

"Has he ever held office before?"

"Why does he believe that he'll be the better candidate for the job?"

I don't think that the poor, unassuming guy on the other end of the phone had ever had anyone keep him on the line, let alone ask him a litany of questions. He gracefully directed me to a Web site for the candidate, along with a phone number I could call if I wanted to pose questions to the candidate directly. As I hung up the phone, I was all too aware that I was close to hitting rock bottom.

∼ Diary Entry 28 ∼

I thought about getting my passport renewed today so that if Brad and I wanted to take off to a foreign country on a whim, we would be ready to pack our bags and jet off to paradise. You never know when you'll win a trip to Italy or Bermuda, and you should always be prepared. Yet, after standing on the scale this morning, I thought it would be best to wait until I shed at least 15 of these unwanted pounds that had crept up.

You have heard of the "Freshman Fifteen" that you gain during your freshman year at college due to the extra intake of pizza and beer? Well, this must be the "Frustrated Fifteen" that one gains when one is trying hopelessly to become domesticated. I figured that if this passport picture is going to be shown for the next ten years, I don't want the early 2000s to be deemed "The Decade of the Double Chin!"

∼ Diary Entry 29 ∼

In our search for a prospective agent for Jessica, we've already received several polite "Thank you, but no thank you" letters. Don't these people know talent when it shows up in front of them in an 8×10 glossy? I may be partial, but I am confident that Jessica has what it takes to be a star.

Why don't I become her agent? Who better to represent her than her own flesh and blood? Why had I not thought about that sooner? I have several friends who are aspiring actors. I could represent them also, while I'm at it. I had been an investment broker, so, what could be so different about brokering people? Here I go again…I am supposed to be retired. Not learning a new industry. Not creating a new venture. No, no, no. These "coaching sessions" with myself seem to be happening more frequently.

∼ Diary Entry 30 ∼

Zachary joined a T-ball league and practices began today. So, I was given the honor of shopping for his first pair of cleats and athletic cup. I must have looked a little intimidated by the wall of athletic supporters, because a sales guy approached as I was biting my fingernails.

"What size do you need?"

"Well, he's five years old," I explained.

"Do you need soft cup or hard cup?" he probed.

"I don't know. He'll be playing baseball, so what would you suggest?" I questioned.

"Hard cup," he said emphatically and shoved a small white package into my hands.

My cheeks were flushed. I know that millions of people buy them each year, but it just seemed to me that it was something that Brad should have handled. But, I was the one who was not working, so it only made sense that I take care of it. While I was at it, maybe I should have gone to purchase some condoms and feminine hygiene products to complete my day?

∼ Diary Entry 31 ∼

Michael, my brother, called today and asked if I'd decorate the reception area of his and Brad's office. I didn't hesitate. I jumped at the opportunity to fill my day with something productive. (I measure productivity by having a tangible outcome to show for one's efforts.)

I was elated at the thought of transforming their barren reception area into an inviting oasis. My vision was quickly stifled when Brad announced, "I'll give you five hundred dollars to do the decorating."

"Five hundred dollars?!" I laughed. "What do you want, lawn chairs in there?"

My husband knows full and well that $500 would not even cover a coffee table, let alone a couch, rug, art, etc. My only theory was that he was negotiating in reverse. If he started at one-tenth of what he thinks

I would spend, then I'd end up closer to his number than my own. What he should have known was that his wife is not a bargain shopper. Michael said, "How about a thousand dollars? They transform rooms for a thousand dollars on those makeover shows."

I calmly explained that on those shows, they have furniture to refurbish or to recover. Not a barren reception area! They both fell silent. I took this as a green light to begin my quest for redesigning their space. I thought I had won that battle; but in retrospect, Brad probably figured that if I was going to be out there shopping, he might as well have something to show for it.

I had been away from corporate America for one month now, and my two biggest fears had been realized. First, I was losing my ability to recognize when I was being manipulated. Second, my shopping was relegated to bargain basements and discount stores. The horror!

∼ Diary Entry 32 ∼

After a long day of scouring the town for rugs and sofas for the guys' office, I was whipped. There was no way that I was going to be able to do the impossible. So, I set a reasonable number in my head that would serve as the "revised budget" and decided to go from there. What are they going to do, fire me? They just need to remind themselves that they had chosen not to hire a professional. Instead, they had hired a stay-at-home mom with a shopping dependency. You get what you pay for.

∼ Diary Entry 33 ∼

What a great day. I decided that after dragging myself around town, armed with fabric swatches and paint chips, I deserved to treat myself to a massage. There is nothing better than letting yourself slip away for one hour and have your body and mind relax to their full potential. I left the spa feeling like I was reborn and that I had purchased a slice of heaven. My limbs were like Jell-O. My state was sheer bliss. I drove my new Zen-like self to pick up Zachary from school. We came home and did our ritual of snack time, coloring, and homework.

When it came time to pick up Jessica from school, Zachary asked, "Can we take the cat in the car to pick up Jessica?"

"Sure we can!" I said on a whim. I like being spontaneous, and in my relaxed state, he could have asked me for a year's supply of chocolate, and I would have complied. We get to Jessica's school (we being Zachary, myself, and our kitten, Abbey), and while waiting for the dismissal bell to ring, Zach is squirming all over the car.

"Zach, what's the matter? Why can't you sit still?" I ask.

"I have to go potty," he moans.

"Why didn't you go before we left the house?" I reason.

"I didn't have to go *then!*"

"Well, we have Abbey with us, so we can't go into the school building. Can you hold it until Jessica gets out in two minutes?" I plead.

"Yes, I can hold it," he said.

Then we waited, with Zach in the backseat writhing with the discomfort of a full bladder and the cat meowing at the top of her lungs. Jessica showed up a few minutes later, but it seemed as if we had been parked for a week.

"Can you watch the cat while I take your brother inside to use the bathrooms?" I said.

Before she could answer, Zachary said, "I can hold it until we get home."

"Are you sure?" I demanded.

He seemed confident in his answer, and he also seemed distracted by playing with the cat. So, I headed home. On the way, Jessica was telling me about her day, and I made some comment that the kids found hysterical.

We laughed and giggled and were enjoying the time, when all of a sudden, Zachary yelled, "Mommy, why did you make me laugh? You made me pee!"

My laughter screeched to a halt, although Jessica found it extremely amusing. So, there I sat, at a red light, just 30 seconds from our home, with a frightened kitten, a mortified five-year-old, a teasing teenager, and a puddle of urine on my leather seats. My Zen-like peace had evaporated into thin air—air that had a musty odor.

∼ Diary Entry 34 ∼

Today, I was asked by the "Team Mom" for Zach's T-ball league to fill in for her in the dugout. She explained, "It is no big deal. The kids just need their helmets and bats, and you send them out there to play." I told her that I'd be happy to help her out.

"No big deal," my ass! Here were 13 children ranging in ages from four to six years old. It was like trying to herd kangaroos.

"Okay, you guys, you need to sit in your batting order so I can get you ready to bat," I said. Utter chaos and pandemonium was still the response. Two of the boys were pushing each other; one boy was leaving the cage to follow a rabid, stray dog; another little boy was climbing the side of the cage; and yet another was rocking back and forth, hugging himself.

"Really, you guys, I need for you to listen so we can beat the other team. You guys want to win, right?" I implored, appealing to their primal need to compete. Apparently, that primal need doesn't kick in for a few years. I received slightly more cooperation but not much.

They calmed down to the point that they did not have to be sedated but still rowdy enough that I briefly thought about needing a stiff drink in the middle of the day. After the second inning, they were back in full form.

"I have treats for everyone who sits down and waits for their turn to bat," I announced. Bribery is such a wonderful motivator. They ran back to their assigned spots and allowed me to outfit them to go take their respective turns at bat. True, some had the wrong helmets, and others were hitting for the first time with a teammate's equipment, but there was no bloodshed.

"Here's your Tootsie Pop, and yours, and yours," I chimed as they left the dugout. The bag of treats was the best $2.00 investment that I had ever made. Give me corporate vipers any day over a bunch of sugared-up children. The vipers are much more predictable and less scary.

∿ Diary Entry 35 ∿

Speaking of scary, we spent the night huddled in a closet, trying to escape the first hurricane to hit Central Florida in over 40 years. There we were, me, Jess, Zach, the two cats and dog, in a 5×6-foot space. Brad spent most of the time peeking his head outside to witness the 110-mile-per-hour winds for himself. There is definitely a testosterone thing with men and storms. We dutifully listened to our handheld radio and ate snacks by flashlight. Outside we could hear the unrelenting winds whirling over our roof and slamming against our windows like an unwelcome intruder.

We awoke to no electricity or running water, but we were all safe and sound. Then we began the cleanup of the devastation that met us outside. Branches and roof shingles were everywhere. Large trees, with root structures eight feet wide, were pulled from the ground as if they were herbs in a garden. Our majestic oak tree had splintered like flimsy driftwood and had fallen in our driveway. If I had had the foresight to know which direction it was going to fall, I would have parked my BMW under it to finally put it and myself out of our misery!

∼ Diary Entry 36 ∼

We are still without electricity or water. How spoiled we all are for modern conveniences like bathing and cooking. In the weeks prior to Hurricane Charlie, I had secretly been wishing that I'd never see a pot or pan again. Had I prayed too hard? Maybe I wasn't the only one praying for my domestic servitude to end. Maybe this hurricane was some type of collective consciousness thing brought on by Mother Nature standing up for her girls who were being held prisoner by their respective kitchens. Well, I wouldn't have time to think about this or other theories, as work and school had been canceled for the foreseeable future. With a house full of kids and husband, gone was any hope for solitude.

∼ Diary Entry 37 ∼

I survived my second major trip to Michael's arts and crafts. The shelves were almost as barren as the post-hurricane grocery store shelves. It seems I was not the only mother with the same idea to busy the hands of their little ones. If they were holding a paintbrush, it was hard for them to be dressing up our dog in doll's clothes or shoving pennies in the VCR. So, we returned home to paste, paint, and cut by flashlight. I pondered if this is how the pioneers became so handy?

∼ Diary Entry 38 ∼

The kids are still off from school due to the hurricane. However, with the extensive damage our city suffered, there are not too many establishments open for business. It's got to be the closest thing to being on "House Arrest." As the power company crews are working tirelessly to restore power to Greater Orlando, I am working tirelessly to keep my children entertained. Who says that this is not a full-time job?

∼ Diary Entry 39 ∼

Hallelujah! We have power! A huge wave of relief swept over my body. They have announced that the kids' schools will be opening the following day. Here's to the three R's of Reading, wRiting, and Relaxing! (The latter being for Mom, not the kids.)

I laughed at a fleeting thought I had earlier this summer about home schooling the kids. It might be a good fit for some, but I was convinced I did not have the patience or the energy to keep up with them 24/7. It would be a classic "Lose/Lose" situation for all involved (with the exception of Jess and Zach being able to list things on their college applications like "Class President" or being voted "Most likely to succeed"). We would, however, be able to keep our relationships intact and not have to resort to any over-the-counter drugs.

∼ Diary Entry 40 ∼

Ah, time to myself. Well, not exactly. Zachary's birthday party is tomorrow, and I spent the day taking care of last-minute items like making the cake, getting prizes for the games, ordering a moonwalk in the shape of a pirate, and preparing goody bags.

I had to remind myself that I was the one who insisted on the old-fashioned, at-home birthday party. At the end of the day, I was convinced that Martha Stewart deserved to be jailed. The insider trading for which she was found guilty paled in comparison to the unrealistic expectations she set for millions of housewives. Keep her behind bars, I say. She makes the rest of us mere mortals look bad.

∼ Diary Entry 41 ∼

Zach's big day was a hit with him and his friends. They had a blast dressing like pirates, playing games, swimming, bouncing, rolling, biting, crawling, etc. I was not sure if it was fueled by excitement or by the perpetual sugar-induced high of the candy, cake, and ice cream.

By the end of the party, I was glad to have it behind me. Hurricane Charlie was no match for the three-hour power surge we endured from the 19 six-year-olds who descended on our home. Next year, Chuck E. Cheese's will be getting the honor of ringing in the big "seven" for Zach's birthday bash. I must admit, that giant rodent is better equipped than I to handle it.

∼ Diary Entry 42 ∼

I can't believe my eyes. The weather stations are predicting *another* hurricane to hit Central Florida! Hurricane Frances is just east of the coast, ready to pummel our shores. Here we go again…

∼ Diary Entry 43 ∼

Motherhood has definitely prepared me for this storm season because it teaches you that everything is relative. Once you experience a child cutting off their own bangs, you realize that it's better than if they had cut off a finger; at least the hair will grow back.

Or once you have had a child who has been given detention for a rare indiscretion, you realize that it's better than if they had been expelled from school. So, as we received 90-mile-an-hour winds and torrential rain of this category three Hurricane Francis, I saw that it was better than if she had been packing a category five punch. Thank God for kids.

∼ Diary Entry 44 ∼

After the posttraumatic stress we endured due to Mother Nature, Brad and I decided to take a trip to get away. We had arranged for Jessica to stay with her best friend's family, and Zach had been "farmed out" to Beth and Jeff, friends of ours who have a son Zach's age. We wanted a brief yet romantic weekend getaway to a picturesque winery and spa in Georgia. (Yeah, I know, winemaking in Georgia…who'd have thought it? The Napa Valley of the South.)

Chateau Élan was to be our oasis. Little did we know that the last hurricane, which had miraculously missed Orlando, was now headed toward our Georgia retreat. What are the odds? Any more water and I am going to have to start lining up the animals two by two! So, we went anyway because the tickets and room were nonrefundable and because I reasoned that at least somebody else would have to be cleaning up the hurricane debris while we were being buffed, polished, wrapped, and rubbed.

After a somewhat relaxing stay (we were placed on a floor with a giant bridal party who did a great impersonation of drunken college students on their first Spring Break), we headed home. We stopped off to pick up Zachary first. I knew that a six-year-old has a much shorter stay of welcome than a 13-year-old. I half expected Beth and Jeff to open the door bleary-eyed and looking like they had just gone 11 rounds in the ring with a heavyweight champion. Instead, our friends were smiling, laughing, and Zach had made himself right at home.

"Can I live with them *forever*?" Zach yelled to us as our welcome home greeting. It's not bad enough that Beth is bright and talented, and Jeff is witty and looks like Adonis; but now, after two short days, Zach wanted to abandon us for them.

"Didn't you miss us?" I asked gently.

"Not really," Zach answered honestly. "We went to a soccer game, ate pizza, and went swimming at the country club!" he said, struggling to think of the rest of his itinerary.

"Well, it sounds like you had fun," Brad chimed in, "but it's time to leave now."

"Ohhh, man!" was Zach's response. So he hung his head low as he was forced to leave paradise.

Next, we swung by to pick up Jessica. Although she was glad to see us, her first response was, "Why did you get Zachary before me?"

On some level, it was nice to know that if Brad and I died in a tragic car accident, our kids would not be emotionally scarred for life. On another level, I was hurt that we were so easily replaced! The only thing that eased my mind was that staying a short period with friends is somewhat like dating. You are on your best behavior. It's not until the relationship gets comfortable that you stop shaving your legs each day, or you stop putting the toilet seat down. Our friends and kids had just experienced the child-watching equivalent of dating. No, our kids really didn't want a new mom and dad; they just liked the "newness" of the relationship. Well, even if that isn't the case, they are stuck with us for the meantime!

∼ Diary Entry 45 ∼

One of the neighborhood kids dropped by today to play with Zachary…at 7:15 a.m.! Don't his parents know that he is out giving early morning wake-up calls to unsuspecting families? Or, maybe these are the smart mothers who send their kids out of the house at the crack of dawn so they can enjoy their morning coffee without having to have the first words of the day that they utter be "Put down those scissors! If you cut off the cat's whiskers, she won't be able to measure spaces to fit through!"

∼ Diary Entry 46 ∼

We went over to the in-laws for a family get-together. Not known for my culinary skills, I am usually in charge of bringing the wine or the nap-kins—two jobs that don't require any cooking or baking. My mother-in-law was busy preparing dinner in the kitchen. I wandered in there and asked if there was anything I could do to help. (Note: The majority of the dinner was already fixed, so this isn't as altruistic as it sounds.)

"Sure," she said. "Can you put out some crackers on the cheese tray?"

"No problem," I responded cheerfully. "What type of crackers do you want me to put out?"

"Oh, you decide," she answered.

Wow, really, I can decide? This is where my life has led me? For a woman who once made hundreds of investment decisions a day that would affect the fate of many futures, I was now in charge of deciding whether or not to have Wheat Thins vs. cracked pepper wafers with the cheese? I went with the Wheat Thins.

∼ Diary Entry 47 ∼

I had taken a hiatus from doing crafts with the kids. There are only so many things that you can do with a Popsicle stick. So, I changed gears, and we have been playing board games. Yes, that's the answer. When we were young, we didn't have Game Boys, CD-ROM, and all this technology. No sir, we played games like "Twister," "Life," and "Chutes and Ladders." So, today, I dusted off my "Candy Land" and set out to turn back the hands of time. Zachary and I played several games. He was quite good. I wasn't even trying to throw the game his way, and he had already won four out of four games. As we were getting ready to play our fifth and final game, I saw him take the "Queen Frostine" card out of the deck.

He was palming it in his cute little cheating hand. "Hey!" I squawked. "What do you think you are doing? You are a Cheater, Cheater, Pumpkin Eater!" He looked at me incredulously and replied as if outraged, "I am NOT a Pumpkin Eater!" Who says that the moral fiber of a family increases with the presence of a stay-at-home mom?

⌒ Diary Entry 48 ⌒

Shopping has always been a great release for me. Some people play tennis, and some people write poetry to unwind. My release is found at the mall. That was the case until I started shopping with a teenager. My mom has got to be laughing at me and not with me, because I remember her words like it was yesterday.

"Some day, *you* will have a daughter, and *you* will know what it is like!"

So, today I found myself chanting things like, "No, Jessica, you can not get those pants. Not until you are eighteen and can legally vote… No, Jessica, that shirt is a little too revealing. That is, unless you have started your career as an exotic dancer and have not informed me." God definitely has a twisted sense of humor.

⌒ Diary Entry 49 ⌒

Today, I started to day-trade investments. For years, I had counseled many clients that asset allocation and "long-term investments" are the prudent way to build wealth. Suddenly, prudent didn't seem so exciting. I used to preach to friends when they shared their latest conquests about an individual stock they were trading in and out of on a regular basis. I tried to reason with them by saying, "Day-trading is nothing more than glorified gambling!" Well, here I sit, punching keys on my computer, looking for my next suitable stock pick. Maybe tomorrow I will hit the dog tracks and a few bingo halls.

ᕲ Diary Entry 50 ᕲ

My whole life seems to revolve around errands and shuttling the kids to their activities. I am in and out of the car more than a FedEx delivery guy. We have school drop-off; we have baseball practice; we have baseball games; we have after-school clubs; we have dance; we have drama club; we have auditions, and we have play dates. Couple that with grocery shopping and dry-cleaning runs, and you have an accurate picture of how I am putting my hard-earned college degree to work. I am an unpaid taxi driver. I swear, if I installed a meter to track the "fares" I am racking up, I could afford a second home. Yeah, yeah, I know...be thankful that my kids are involved in activities instead of being introverts. All I know is that the one place I *won't* mind taking them to is to the driver's license bureau on the day that they turn 16!

ᕲ Diary Entry 51 ᕲ

Part of the privilege of being a grown-up is that we no longer have nightly homework assignments from school. We paid our dues along the way and did our fair share of quadratic equations and solar system models made from little Styrofoam balls. So, when Jessica approached me tonight for help in her math class, I was caught completely off-guard.

"Mom," she whined, "I can't figure out these problems, and they are due tomorrow!" She is in eighth-grade algebra, and I figured, although I have never enjoyed math, surely, I could lend my daughter a helping hand. I stared at the page she handed me, as the four problems on the sheet of paper might as well have been written in an ancient foreign language.

"*This* is eighth-grade math?" I pondered, as I was trying to formulate a way to let her know that her mother, who spent seven years as a successful investment advisor, is incapable of doing her homework, while still being able to hang onto some of my self-respect.

"Why don't you get your dad to help you with it?" I suggested. "He has always been a whiz at math."

"I already *did* ask him for help. He doesn't understand it, either!" So, now, not only did she think that I got my college degree from a Cracker Jack box, but she thinks we got a two-for-one special.

"Well, it has been soooo many years since either of us has done this type of problem. It's not like riding a bike," I reason. "You can't expect us to hop back on after all these years."

"Ugh, you guys are no help!" she groaned as she left our room, shaking her head back and forth.

"We love you, Jessica!" I yelled to her as she climbed the stairs to her room. That's got to count for something. Apparently, that's the only thing I could count on lately, since my abacus had been put out to pasture.

∼ Diary Entry 52 ∼

"How's retirement going?" crooned friends who called to check on me. How could I tell them that I longed for the rat race I once talked about with such disdain? "Oh, it's great," I lied. I would rather have been sitting at my desk, putting out the proverbial "fire" than cleaning up hurricane debris, as well as mounds of shit from an un-housebroken dog.

"I envy you," they would sigh. "You don't know how lucky you are not to have to work."

Why didn't I feel lucky? Why didn't I leap out of bed each morning to welcome the new day? Why had I been regretting my decision to stay home full-time? Why do they not put erasers at the end of Putt-Putt golf pencils? Well, I needed to find the answers to at least the first three questions.

CHAPTER 3

LATER DIARY ENTRIES

∿ Diary Entry 53 ∿

I finally took off my "Super Mom" outfit and confided in my best friend Julie that I am going stir-crazy. It seems like an awful confession, the fact that being a full-time mom isn't enough for me. We have known each other since fifth grade, so anything I say shouldn't surprise her. Regardless of the fact, I braced myself for a lecture on "why I should stop being so selfish" or the benefits of getting with "the program." Instead, she shared with me about *her* feelings after she left the workforce. She assured me that it's normal to have these emotions. She went on to tell me details of times during her first year at home with the kids when she felt like she was going to be committed to a padded white cell.

"Are you serious," I asked. "Or are you just saying this to make me feel like less of a self-centered bitch?" She assured me that I was not alone. Does that mean I am not alone in having these feelings of self-doubt about my maternal instinct or not alone in being a self-centered bitch? She assured me that it was the former of the two and let me in on a little secret: Thousands, possibly millions of women struggle with sorting through all the roles we are expected to manage: "Mother," "Wife," "Friend," "Daughter," "Breadwinner," "Lover," "Maid," "Chauffeur," and "Social Planner." Where is our true identity in all of these roles? Where have we buried our true self? Where indeed?

∿ Diary Entry 54 ∿

After my talk yesterday with Julie, I knew that I needed to look outside my home life for hobbies. What could I pursue to help fill that feeling of dissatisfaction I was experiencing? Hmmm. Needlepoint? Painting? Scuba diving? No, none of these were on my "Top 100 Things To Do Before I Die" list. This is an actual list, which I created about eight years ago.

A friend of mine had died of breast cancer at the age of 31, and it was a tremendous wake-up call for me. The realization set in that we are not immortal. I embraced the fact that I had to start living my life like each day could be my last. I acknowledged the fact that when people say, "I'll be able to do that *someday*, when I have the time or money" that their day may never come. All we have is today.

So, I went about listing all the things I wanted to learn, experience, and do while I am still alive. The items were spiritual, financial, emotional, or recreational. They ranged from taking sax lessons, to learning a second language, to entertaining friends and family more frequently, to having a second child. (The last one came true six years ago when we had Zachary.) Starting a children's charity was also on my list. Hence, The Golden Rule Foundation was born five years ago as a direct result of cataloguing my life's dreams and desires. Yes, it was time to revisit the list.

∼ Diary Entry 55 ∼

I contacted the Delta Aviation Academy today to sign up for flying lessons! After all, it was number one on my list of things to do before I die. I was extremely excited. I phoned a few friends to tell them what I had done.

"Aren't you enough of a threat in a car?" they teased.

Others noted, "I have white knuckles when I drive with you."

It's amazing that a few tickets and a handful of minor fender benders can mark you forever as a bad driver. Nonetheless, I am determined to get my private pilot's license. I envision jetting off for a romantic getaway in the Bahamas. I dream of taking off, on a whim, to meet friends in West Palm Beach for dinner. I feel less like a caged animal already.

∼ Diary Entry 56 ∼

Halloween is here, and it is, bar none, my favorite holiday of the year. Call it the "Peter Pan" syndrome if you like. I just love the idea of playing make-believe. In college, I would start thinking about what I was going to be for Halloween several months in advance. Brad would also get strong-armed into dressing up. To say that he was a good sport about it was a big understatement. One year, he was the angel to my devil. Another year, he was Bert to my Ernie. (Sesame Street is timeless.) After being dressed in tights for a few years, he put his foot down and demanded to be dressed in something a bit more masculine. Gradually, he grabbed better "roles" as a gangster and the Big Bad Wolf.

So, needless to say, when they had parents sign up to help with Zachary's Halloween party, my name was at the top of the list. The big day arrived, and Zachary asked if I was going to dress up when I came to his school at lunchtime.

"Do you want me to?" I asked, hoping silently that he would say yes.

"Of course I want you to!" he squealed. I let out a sigh of relief. With kids, you get to use them as an excuse to let your inner child run with abandoned freedom.

"Okay," I said. "I'll see you later at your party." As I dropped my little vampire off, with his bat in one hand and lunchbox in the other, I noticed that very few teachers were dressed in costumes.

"Hmmm," I thought. "Well, maybe they are waiting until party time to get changed." I went home to start getting ready. By lunchtime, I had transformed myself into a five-foot, five-inch giant sunflower, complete with a foam terra-cotta pot and moss. I drove to the school with my face painted black and giant yellow petals protruding from my convertible. The costume was so large that I had to put it on in stages.

As I put the finishing touches on my enormous pot, I glanced at the other mothers bringing in their trays of cookies and cupcakes. Not one was dressed in a costume. You would have thought from looking around that it was just any ordinary Friday. They nodded at me and said things like, "Oh, how cute!" and "How adorable!" Most kept their comments to themselves. I suspected that they needed to in order to stifle their laughter.

Suddenly, dressing up in a costume when nobody else was didn't seem as much fun. I momentarily thought about turning around, but I knew that Zachary would get a good laugh. So, I bravely walked down the corridors with my leaves swaying side to side and made my way to where Zach's class was out on the playground. True, a few teachers had on Dr. Seuss hats and others wore witches hats, but nobody was in full regalia! Nobody, that was, except me.

I approached Zachary and said, "Ta Da!" He looked at me without acknowledgment and went on swinging from the monkey bars. He either didn't recognize me, or he *did* and will need years of therapy on a psychologist's couch from this episode. I opted to believe that he didn't know who I was.

"Zachary!" I chirped. "It's *me*, Mommy!"

"Mommy? It doesn't even look like you!" he laughed. He paraded me around, holding my hand, and showed me off to the kids in his class. "Look, my mom's a flower!" he said proudly. "What did your mom dress up as?" he asked a little girl with cute blond ringlets, dressed as Tinkerbell.

I wanted to say, "She dressed like an uptight, undersexed housewife." But I bit my tongue. Not everybody was as obsessed with Halloween as I was.

What I realized today, as I stood out in 90-degree sweltering weather (dressed as a gigantic black-eyed Susan), was that I was glad that I had just created a memory for my son that he was not going to forget. The flip side of that was neither were the other mothers. Well, maybe it will leave them with the message of the fun you are capable of having when you don't take life too seriously.

∼ Diary Entry 57 ∼

Following my theme of having as much fun as possible and living life to its fullest, I planned a dinner party for a few close friends. Again, I didn't let the fact that I don't know how to cook stop me. I started at the crack of dawn, and by seven o'clock that night, I had enough overcooked beef to feed eight people.

Luckily, I had given the dinner party a theme of "Wine Country." So, with each overdone course, I had paired a wine or cordial. By the third course, I don't think that anyone knew what he or she was eating, let alone that it was inedible. Here's to strong libations or finding out just how far you can stretch a friendship.

∼ Diary Entry 58 ∼

For years I have lived in a very subtly decorated home. We had chosen neutral tones for our home. Our walls were "eggshell" (just another way to explain off-white), our carpet was beige, and our furniture was also in the tan family. So, today, I decided that I would let a part of my personality shine through in the way that I chose to decorate.

I hired a painter and knew that by the end of the day, my bedroom would be anything but plain vanilla. I'd told Brad that I wanted to redecorate our room, but I hadn't shared with him that the new color of our walls would be crimson red.

As he watched our painter put on the first few swipes of color, he looked at me and said, "Are you sure about the color?"

"Trust me!" I replied, as our walls looked like a scene from a graphic murder movie. When the final coat was painted, I stepped back and grinned from ear to ear. This bedroom no longer said "pristine" and "discreet." This bedroom screamed "passion" and "heat." Maybe that's why Brad let me have my way? He would have agreed to live in a room that looked like a brothel as long as it meant more sex!

∼ Diary Entry 59 ∼

Since I had inadvertently almost treated my friends to food poisoning the other night, Holly, a neighborhood friend, suggested that we take a few cooking classes at William's-Sonoma. She's already quite an accomplished cook, so I think the offer for her to go with me was meant as moral support. Knowing that I had a huge sweet tooth (her husband is my cardiologist), she lured me with the offer that we would be making desserts. Well, not technically making them. We watched Peatro, a jovial Italian man with broken English, make them, and we sat back and ate an assortment of five or six exquisite, high-caloric masterpieces. If I'd known that "cooking classes" were this much fun, I would have started years ago. Now, I just have to find the right balance between acquiring new skills for the kitchen and putting on so much extra weight that I don't lose skills in other important rooms in our house.

∼ Diary Entry 60 ∼

From the moment that little boys realize they have a penis, they are intrigued with the apparatus. If I didn't know better, I would say that somebody superglued Zachary's hand in his pants. Knowing that I would probably be getting a friendly note from his school any day now, letting me know that he spends more time with "himself" than practicing his ABCs, I sat him down for an earnest talk.

"Zach, do you remember how we talked about our private parts?" I gently asked.

"Yes," he answered.

"Well," I bumbled on, "it's something that we do in private. When you touch yourself in public, it can make people feel uncomfortable. That is something that you can do alone in your room."

He looked at me and shook his head with dismay and replied, "But, Mom, there's just not enough time during the day to play with it!"

All these years of trips to Toys "R" Us to buy basketball nets and bicycles, and it took me being at home to realize that his favorite toy could not be purchased in a store…priceless.

∼ Diary Entry 61 ∼

I discovered another Mommy secret today: The coveted "play date." A mom from Zachary's class called and asked if Zach could come over and play with her son for a few hours. So, I packed up Zach, drove him across town, and dropped him at a virtual stranger's house.

"Just pick him up in a few hours," she said.

A few hours to myself without having to entertain another human being? Yippee! What would I do first? Well, since it was last minute, it was too late to call a friend to meet for lunch. No, just being given 120 minutes of unexpected free time was a treasure in and of itself. I felt like a kid at Christmas. I came home, ran a hot bubble bath, and read a book that had been in my drawer for ages. Play dates to the rescue!

∼ Diary Entry 62 ∼

I found out today that there is no such thing as a "free lunch." The mother from Zach's play date yesterday phoned and asked if her son could come to our house and play today.

"Sure!" I said. "We'd be happy to have him come over."

Minutes later there was a freckle-faced six-year-old at our doorstep. They scampered upstairs and kept themselves busy playing with Legos, Lincoln Logs, and Transformers.

As they played, I thought to myself, "Wow! This is like having *another* day of freedom. They are keeping each other entertained."

That thought was dispelled when Zach ran into the room and announced, "Brandon is bleeding!"

"Bleeding?! What happened? Is he all right?" I shrieked, as I sprinted up the stairs two at a time. It turned out that it wasn't worthy of an emergency room visit, just a cut finger on a sharp toy. No harm, no foul. Well, virtually little harm.

Hopefully, this would not ruin our play date arrangement. I mean, does a small amount of bloodshed mean you don't get a second date? And what are the other rules and etiquette for play dates? Are you expected to phone the next day and say you had a good time? Can you see other people, or are you expected to date them exclusively? So much to learn, but I had the time.

∼ Diary Entry 63 ∼

I had my first flying lesson today. I am hooked! Initially, I was scared shitless; but by the time the plane landed, I knew what it felt like to be a bird. In a small plane, you truly can feel the wind beneath your wings. It was a very spiritual experience, communing with nature and God all at once. I can't wait to get enough hours so that I can fly by myself.

The second benefit of the flight lesson is that I don't have to join Jenny Craig for weight loss. Part of prepping for your flight is doing what they call a "weight and balance." You have to put down your weight and that of your instructor, in addition to the plane itself, fuel, etc. This is going to be like a public, biweekly weigh-in. Talk about multitasking!

∼ Diary Entry 64 ∼

Brad and I met for lunch today. For years, we worked in the same office building and rarely saw each other during the day. So, it was a nice treat to put aside time to meet when we didn't have to referee arguments between the kids or scream over the dog barking in order to hear how the other person's day had gone. It was almost reminiscent of when we first started dating (without the undertone of thinking, "I wonder what he looks like naked?"). We laughed and talked, and before we knew it, he had to get back to his office. It was so refreshing to have a conversation without interruptions from telephone solicitors.

∼ Diary Entry 65 ∼

Knowing how good it felt to reconnect with my husband, I decided to write a few letters and make a few phone calls to catch up with some old friends. It's funny how busy our lives get, and we don't slow down enough to nurture ourselves or the relationships that help us define who we are. After a few hours of hearing about upcoming weddings, new jobs, new boyfriends, and new hobbies for their kids, I felt like I was a new woman. I had forgotten how good it feels to share in other people's excitement. There was hope for me yet.

∼ Diary Entry 66 ∼

Life should be about unexpected surprises. With that thought in mind, I told Jessica last night that she did not have to go to school today. (Truancy officers be damned!) Today was her day to be "Boss." She was going to be able to choose what we did all day long. She was in control of where we went, what we ate, and at what time we should do things. I figured that when you are a teenager and you feel, sometimes, like your voice doesn't matter, what is more empowering than feeling like you are in control? So, she asked if Uncle Mike could come along for our adventure.

She began her day by sleeping in until ten o'clock in the morning. A pleasant change from being woken up at 6:45 a.m. by her alarm. She then decided that she wanted to go ice-skating. So, Mike, Jess, and I went to a local indoor rink (not many outdoor rinks here in Florida), and we virtually had the place to ourselves. I guess other responsible parents had their children *in* school that day. Next, she decided that she wanted to make a "rock video" later in the afternoon.

In order to get into character for the video, we stopped at a Salvation Army thrift store to get our wardrobe. We had a blast picking out spandex pants, fur vests, and beads for our big debut. (Never had I had so much fun shopping for eight dollars!)

When it was lunchtime, instead of going to a restaurant, she chose to go to the grocery store so each of us could buy our favorite foods to eat.

Suffice it to say, there was lots of chocolate involved. We came home, had our sugar fest, and took turns filming each other lip-synching to different hip-hop songs. (Remember to erase the video footage lest it could be used against me in future years.)

She then wanted to go see a movie and go out to Barnes and Noble before the day came to an end. On our way home from the bookstore, she told me with all sincerity, "Mom, this was the best day of my life." Was it worth breaking a rule or two to hear her say that? You bet. I also learned a lot about her character today. She was very diplomatic in her decisions, and she was not demanding. She got to have her way, but she did not take advantage of the situation. She felt respected, and she felt special. She knew that tomorrow, things would be back to normal with her regular routine, but she would go to sleep with the knowledge that she has the power to make good choices for herself and that her mom is always there for her. She learned a lot today, and she hadn't been in school.

∿ Diary Entry 67 ∿

I took off midweek to go down to Boca Raton to celebrate my Uncle Corky's 75th birthday (something that I would not have done if I had still been working). Uncle Corky has been such a driving force in my life. He was my father figure after my dad passed away shortly after I graduated from college. I cherish my aunt and uncle as much as I love and cherish my mom. So, I was glad that I could be there to help him celebrate his life. (In addition to being there for him, there was an added benefit for me of looking like a hottie next to the sea of ladies with blue hair!)

As we drank cocktails and dined in a small banquet room with 50 or so of his close friends and relatives, I was so heart-warmed by all the lives that he had touched. I can only hope that my life can be a gift to many others.

∿ Diary Entry 68 ∿

I spent most of the day driving back to Orlando from South Florida. As I drove on the turnpike, I thought about what I wanted to do with the rest of my life. Would I start a career again? (After listening to myself singing off-key to the radio for the last few hours, it certainly won't be a career in music.) What did I want for myself? What did I want for my family? Even though I haven't come up with a definitive answer to my questions, I do know that I have been given the power to create what I choose to envision.

∼ Diary Entry 69 ∼

Along the lines of creating something for my family, I wanted to start a tradition. Growing up, I remember little traditions, like when we were sick, we were given a small brass bell to ring, and, like magic, my mom appeared by our bedside each time it rang. So, the bell thing was taken, but there were other possibilities. I wanted to create a symbol of love and caring. I wanted to have a reminder for each of us that we were an integral part of one another's lives.

We sat around the dinner table, and I asked the kids and Brad if they wanted to start a family tradition. I told them about my idea that we should choose an object and whoever possesses the object, that person would do something nice for another member of the family. In turn, the family member that had just received the object would choose somebody else to surprise with a nice gesture. The acts of kindness were just that. Money did not have to be spent. It could be something as simple as making someone's bed, leaving someone a love note, or giving someone a back rub. Jessica selected a tiny stuffed animal of hers, and hence, "Snuggles" was born. Brad will be the first to have Snuggles to give away. I can't wait to see what he will do with it.

∼ Diary Entry 70 ∼

Death is difficult to deal with at any age, but it is especially hard for kids. Today, Zach's turtle died. If it wasn't hard enough watching the tears stream down his face when he discovered the turtle floating upside-down in his tank, even harder was the fact that he had named the turtle "Zachary Junior." Now we were faced with having to flush his namesake down the toilet.

I don't know why my kids have both named pets after themselves. When Jessica was his age, we went through five or six "Jessica" goldfish before we told her that the fish was being sent to the "Big Fishbowl in the Sky." Now, I found myself trying to comfort him with hugs and kisses, but Zachary was mourning his loss. He rarely played with the turtle, but now that he didn't have him, I wondered if he was sad about the time he *could* have spent with the turtle but had not done so. What a lesson to learn at the tender age of six.

What a lesson to learn at any age, for that matter. We need to seize each opportunity when it is ours for the taking, or we might end up with a mountain of regrets. We did decide to give Zachary Junior a proper burial. (Well, by "proper," I don't mean to suggest that *I* want to be put in a Ziploc baggie in the ground versus a casket.) We said our good-byes, and Zachary said a prayer out loud.

"Please, God, take care of Zachary Junior for me and make sure he is okay. Amen."

Uncle Mike then took him to the pet store to get Zachary Junior II.

∾ Diary Entry 71 ∾

Brad surprised Jessica today with Snuggles. He woke her up early (that part wasn't so special since she is a teenager who would ordinarily like to sleep to noon each day if she could) and took her out for a Daddy/Daughter breakfast prior to taking her to school. They spent an hour of uninterrupted time, talking and catching up with no baby brother or Mom to compete for his attention. He found out how her classes were going and the upcoming play she was trying out for. I am not sure if she shared about her current crush, but all good things come in time. Besides, Brad knows with the way she looks, he will have to have a few baseball bats and a gun waiting by our front door when she starts dating. In the meantime, he said that breakfast at Denny's had never tasted so good.

∾ Diary Entry 72 ∾

The public weigh-ins for flying have become enough of an incentive to make me brush off the dust on my YMCA card and put it to good use. I went to the YMCA today for the first time in months. I started on the treadmill and progressed to the stationary bike and pushed on to free weights. I truly felt wonderful. It was the first time that I didn't care that I was surrounded by 20-somethings in peak physical condition. I didn't care that my wrists were the size of their thighs. I was done comparing myself to others. It was high time that I became my own measuring stick. My choice to work out today was a much better choice than running nonsensical errands. Each day, I can either make choices that enhance and elevate my life or choices that deter and downgrade it. I, most definitely and with complete consciousness, choose to enhance it.

∼ Diary Entry 73 ∼

It seems like it's been years since I did something purely selfish. (That's if you don't count locking the door to the bathroom so that I can sit on the toilet in peace.) So, when Liz, a friend of mine who moved out west a couple of years back, asked recently, "Why don't you come visit me in Montana?" I thought to myself, "Self, why shouldn't I? I have no excuse not to come." Brad could handle the kids for a few days (along with able-bodied relatives pitching in).

So, there I was, booking a trip to Montana to see a good friend. I could see it now…No errands; no chores; no kids; no husband; no responsibilities. Can I really do this? It seems too decadent, so Bohemian. I immediately talked with Melissa and asked if she wanted to come to Utopia with me. This trip, she would not be driving! After getting the green light from her husband, we were giddy with the excitement. The mere thought of being free and untethered had us worked into a frenzy. I felt like an inmate that had just been granted parole after 15 years of "hard time." It was a few hours before I came down off my "high" from booking our girls' trip. When I finally settled down, I realized that I was so anxious to go, I hadn't realized that this Florida girl just booked a getaway to the mountains in the dead of winter! That's okay. Moments of solitude and pure bliss, alone with friends, trump freezing my ass off any day.

∼ Diary Entry 74 ∼

This morning, Jessica bestowed Snuggles upon Zachary! Usually, theirs is a love-hate relationship. Zachary idolizes her, but Jessica views him as a pint-sized pest. So, imagine my surprise when Jessica asked to be woken up early in order to fix Zachary a smoothie for his breakfast (a treat she usually fixes for herself and then refuses to share even a drop with her brother). Today, however, the smoothie was all his.

You would have thought that she just given him a new bike. He was thrilled that she had done something special for him. For once, she wasn't teasing him or loathing him. It almost seemed like I was getting the indirect benefits of Snuggles, because I did not have to referee their bickering today. Zachary came running into my room after he had finished his shake and looked at me with a milk mustache and handed me a special bottle of water he had garnished with a strawberry and proclaimed, "Here you go, Mom. I made it especially for you. And do you know what?" he asked with a toothless smile. "I wish every day was Snuggles day!" I let him know that every day *can* be Snuggles day if you take the time to let others know that you care for them. Don't we all deserve a "Snuggle" each day to remind us how much we are loved?

∼ Diary Entry 75 ∼

Speaking of letting people know how much you love them, my sister Jodi just returned to town. She had moved back to Colorado to be with my other sister, Shelly. Although they love each other and would do anything for each other, after a few short months, they realized that they simply couldn't live with one another. So, Jodi was back.

What's the old saying? "You can choose your friends, but you can't choose your family." Our relationship has always been stressed. Her resentment of me started, I guess, when I was born and dethroned her as the youngest daughter. She delights in telling me how she almost got away with smothering me with a pillow when we were little. Fast forward to high school, and that is where she had nothing but contempt for the fact that I was a straight A student, became a cheerleader, and was a class officer, instead of taking the route she did—one of isolation and depression. Since then, she has turned her life around.

Although she is no longer the "black sheep" of the family, my seemingly perfect life grates on her every nerve. To *me*, my life is perfect. There is very little I would change. She, however, thinks it all came effortlessly and without sacrifice, and that is where she is mistaken. I had to work many long hours, away from my kids, to build the businesses I pursued. I had to take risks. I had to change my lifestyle several times. True, I have a husband who adores me, yet don't even get me started on how much effort it takes to make a marriage work. Parenting is certainly not effortless. There are times when I have felt like taking a drive and wanted to just keep driving and not turn back. There are times when I don't know which will come first: losing my temper or losing my sanity. Being a role model and a disciplinarian to young children is not a cakewalk.

Meanwhile, she loves to be the aunt who spoils them with candy, lets them stay up late, and allows my teenaged daughter to drive illegally without a license! So, although I am pretty sure that she has a voodoo doll in my likeness by her bedside, I want to let her know that there is no such thing as a "right" or "wrong" lifestyle; it's whatever works best for you. The sooner she finds that out, the happier she'll be. I just hope she learns the lesson soon, because I don't want her to end up being *my* Zachary Junior.

∼ Diary Entry 76 ∼

I got smart and instead of throwing a dinner party all by myself, I convinced four couples that we should form a "Gourmet Club." This concept is perfect for me or any other domestically-challenged person who prefers to have help cooking. The premise is this: You pick a themed dinner, and each couple brings items to make a dish that would complement the theme. One of the couples hosts the dinner in their home, and all of the couples arrive several hours before dinner to prepare their food and to watch how the other couples are making their dish. It's brilliant! Not only is the stress of making the entire meal off my back, but also for the duration that it takes to get the meal ready, wine is flowing freely. It simply makes everything taste better by the time we make it to the table to eat.

Anyway, the premier dinner of our "Gourmet" Club (and believe me, the term "Gourmet" is used loosely) was held at our home. The theme was French cuisine, and suffice to say, French onion soup and crème brulée were going to be on the menu. Since I didn't have to do the lion's share of the cooking this time, I went to the store to get some decorations for the table to help my guests believe that they were in a quaint bistro somewhere in Paris. I chose some small cards, decorated with the Arc de Triomphe and the Eiffel Tower, to use as place settings, and that is when I saw him. There he was—a 12-inch-high, harlequin-looking statue of a leotard-clad performer with ballet slippers and a beret. Maybe he wasn't authentically French, but he made me laugh. He's perfect, I thought, as my centerpiece! When I arrived home, I had my "French Man" perched on a counter in my kitchen.

When Jessica came in from outside, she said, "What is *that*?"

"It's my centerpiece for the dinner party tonight," I replied.

"He is CREEPY. Can you put him away until everybody gets here?" she pleaded.

"No, I like him, so he stays," I said proudly, defending my new Parisian friend.

From the time everyone arrived, my French guy was the life of the party.

Everyone laughed at him, held him, and posed for pictures with him. They, too, had agreed with Jessica that he was "Creepy," as he is now fondly referred to. So, imagine my surprise as Brad and I got into bed tonight. Right in the middle of our bed, nestled between our comforter and shams, was "Creepy." Holly had tucked him in for the night. As fond as I was of "Creepy," tonight would not turn into a ménage à trois.

∾ Diary Entry 77 ∾

It was time for Zach's annual physical. The pediatrician had been a client of mine when I worked for Merrill Lynch. Our team managed his group's 401(k) program, and he served on the Board of Directors. He had known me as the woman in a sleek suit, giving the PowerPoint presentation about the performance of the small cap arena versus the international markets. Today, however, I was dressed in ripped jeans, a pullover sweater with a stain or two left over from lunch, and my hair in a ponytail, perched high on my head.

As he was giving Zach his exam, he came to the part where he needed to check Zach's "nether regions." The doctor went to unzip Zach's jeans, and Zach proudly stated, "I am not wearing any underwear!" I shifted in my seat uncomfortably and made a mental note not to let him get dressed without some supervision.

"Oh, you go commando?" the doctor teased.

"No, he ordinarily wears underwear. I guess he missed a step today," I said, trying to conjure up what the doctor must be thinking.

"Well, my Aunt Jodi doesn't wear underwear *any* day," Zach shared so matter-of- factly. Now my face was flushed, and I felt myself starting to sweat.

The doctor started to laugh, and I said, "I'm sure that was more information than you needed to know." I half laughed, half choked. "Just for the record," I said, "I *do* wear underwear."

He giggled to himself and mumbled something about this being good blackmail material. (This is just one of the many reasons I will never run for public office.) As we left the building, Zach and I hand in hand, I started to smile. I laughed harder and deeper the more I replayed the conversation in my head. Being at home had definitely taught me to have a sense of humor. Several months ago, I would have been mortified that someone in my business realm thinks members of my family are closet nudists. Now, I am just grateful to have the oppor- tunity to enjoy a good laugh.

∾ Diary Entry 78 ∾

Today, I realized two things. One, I was not lonely enough to talk to tele- phone solicitors anymore; and two, men still live in the dark ages. Just as I was preparing dinner, the phone rings. A husky voice on the other end of the phone asks, "Is Brad Hamman in?"

"Yes he is," I reply, but suspecting that the man is a telemarketer, I further inquire, "Is he expecting your call?"

"No, he is not, but I am sure he will want to hear what I have to say," the caller declared.

"Well, I am *Mrs. Hamman;* is there anything that *I* can help you with?" I say.

"No, I prefer to talk with Mr. Hamman," he continues.

Starting to feel frustrated, I respond, "I am his wife. What is this in reference to?"

"I am calling about refinancing your home," he says with confidence.

"We are not interested," I say without hesitation because we had refinanced just over one year ago, and we were still paying off closing costs (that coupled with the fact that he had already pissed me off).

Just when I thought he could not get any more condescending: "Do *you* work?" he asked snidely.

"Yes, I work," I said with astonishment, as the dryer was beeping in the background to let me know that the 12th load of laundry that day was complete.

"Well, then you should *know* that saving one and a half percent on refinancing your home is a smart decision. That's why I wanted to talk with your husband!" he bellowed.

"Call me crazy, but when did berating the spouse in a cold call become a savvy marketing move?" I exclaimed and promptly slammed down the phone. I was still fuming when Brad emerged from the other room.

"Don't even get me started!" I seethed. After I told him how this clueless guy just managed to insult me as well as give me a Twilight Zone episode of being stuck in the pre-women's lib movement of the 1960s, Brad suggested I redial and speak with his manager. "No, my time is more valuable than that," I reasoned. Well, what do you know, a third thing that I learned today: Having peace of mind and letting go of stress are more important than being right. That's a first.

∼ Diary Entry 79 ∼

Today, I hid Creepy on top of Brad's laundry hamper, peering out of the mound of dirty clothes. I heard him chuckling in his closet as he was getting ready for work. I, along with a foot-tall, papier-mâché doll, had just set the tone for his day.

∼ Diary Entry 80 ∼

Brad planned a romantic night on the town. We had a dinner for two in a trendy (code for cha ching!) restaurant. We had a great meal, too many glasses of wine, and then he whisked me off to the theater. We had seen "Hairspray" in New York and loved it, so he figured the second time around would be just as nice. We laughed, we cried, and that was just on our way from the bar to our seats. We thoroughly enjoyed the show. He was sure to get lucky tonight.

On the way out of the play and into the parking lot, I was trying to walk briskly (a hard task, by the way, in 3½-inch spiked boots). Since I don't get to take my heels out for a spin during the week, I utilize every opportunity to dress to the nines on the weekend. Tonight was a cold

night in Orlando (48 degrees and dropping), and I couldn't get back in
our car fast enough. We had walked quite a distance, and I moaned,
"Where on earth did we park?" He made a sharp left and walked confidently toward our gold Toyota Highlander. He extended his keyless
remote toward the vehicle, and when I heard the locks pop, I jumped
into the front passenger seat. "Ah, warmth!" I thought. I pivoted slightly in my seat to reach back and grab the shoulder strap for the seat belt.
Just as I was buckling myself in, I saw them. There, at my window,
stood a dumbfounded couple in their early thirties. The striking
blonde and her well-dressed date knocked on my window. I cracked
the door slightly, somewhat miffed that the cold air was invading my
cozy space.

"Ummm, you're in our car," they stated, smiling awkwardly, with
their eyes slightly bulging.

"What?" I exclaimed. Just then, I see Brad one aisle over, pointing at
our identical Highlander. "I am sooooo sorry. I thought this was our
car, or I would have never…" I trailed off. As I slunk off, my embarrassment level the only thing higher than my heels, I made my way to
Brad. The couple was good-natured and very calm about a strange,
shivering lady making herself right at home in their car. They were
either very laid back, or they feared that I was a woman who might be
off her meds.

I now sprinted to meet Brad and checked to make sure that in the
backseat of this car, there was Jessica's iPod, discarded "Happy Meal"
toys of Zach's, and a basketball jersey of Brad's. I was never so relieved
to see our backseat so trashed. It's not always the kids that provide me
with memorable instances such as this. I am fully capable of creating
embarrassing moments all by myself.

∼ Diary Entry 81 ∼

Holly called me a few weeks back and asked if I wanted to do a 5K
race/walk with her for breast cancer. I replied that I usually don't run
unless someone is chasing after me with a knife. She assured me that we
could walk and that it would be fun. Never have I used fitness and fun
in the same sentence. I conceded, though, and there I was at six a.m., off
to do my first race. We arrived at the course, and there were thousands

of women—women who looked like race veterans. It was at this point that I envisioned the sun setting on the horizon, and Holly and me being the last stragglers to cross the finish line. However, it was shortly after the shotgun officially started the race that we realized our brisk walk was keeping us near the middle of the pack. We spent the time people-watching, gossiping, and laughing at the fact that a woman on crutches had just passed us by.

When we crossed the finish line (in under an hour, I might add), I felt a wave of excitement. I had just spent my morning doing something that I never thought I would try. Holly had forced me out of my comfort zone, and I loved it. I stared down at the number that was pinned to my shirt and smiled. Number 523 made it official…I was a marathon racer. Well, marathon walker.

∼ Diary Entry 82 ∼

Flying is definitely exhilarating and humbling all wrapped into one. I have never had to study so hard in my life! That includes studying for my Series Seven investment license, one of the most widely failed tests in America. I am trying to cram all this new information into my brain, and it is not easy, but I know it is crucial.

What other sport or hobby is there where a small mistake or miscalculation can send you spiraling to your death? There must be a small part of me that enjoys the danger. This is the same small part that has urged me to try skydiving, river rafting, and mountain climbing. Maybe in my mind, when I am facing the potential of losing my life, I am more grateful for each moment that I have to live it. Twisted and convoluted as it might seem, this "thrill-seeker" who lives inside me convinces me to try new things. I have a quote hanging in my closet, and it is the first thing that I see each morning as I am getting dressed. It says, "Do something each day that scares you." Well, besides facing the mirror each morning stark naked, I try to do at least one *more* thing.

∼ Diary Entry 83 ∼

After groggily brushing my teeth and wearily making lunches for the kids, I took a nice hot shower. I toweled off and wrapped my hair in a towel "crown" that had me feeling like a queen—a queen of a country where showering is coveted and revered. I reach down to get my make-up case, and lo and behold, Creepy's head is sticking out of my case.

Brad had cleverly inserted Creepy into my daily routine. Finding Creepy made me giggle. It was then that I plotted to get Creepy into Holly's house for her to enjoy. She and I were going out to a movie tonight, and since her husband, Greg, was on call, Jessica was set to baby-sit. I bribed Jessica to take Creepy to their house and hide him in their refrigerator. Holly called, laughing, and uttered something about me having way too much time on my hands. It's ironic that now that I do have more time, I'm dedicating more of myself to my family and friends. I was remembering what it was like to be silly and have no agenda but to enjoy making other people smile.

∼ Diary Entry 84 ∼

I've never been one to seek "permission" to do anything. My motto has always been: "Charge ahead and ask for forgiveness later." This has held true in both my personal and professional life. It has allowed me to take risks in my career, and it has also allowed me to shop without guilt. I used to have this internal dialogue when I shopped that went something like this: "Wow, that's a beautiful dress! Let's take a look at the price. Oooh, a little expensive, but hey, I work. I deserve to treat myself to something extravagant once in awhile. I am a hefty contributor to our household's bottom line. This is something that I want, so, I am going to get it."

Well, that conversation now goes something like this: "Wow, what a beautiful dress! Let's take a look at the price. YIKES! What am I think-ing? How can I justify buying this? I don't work anymore, so, I no longer contribute to our finances. Where would I even wear a beautifully embroidered Kay Unger cocktail dress?" This is the part in the conver-sation where I pause and notice my fellow shoppers staring at me while I stand in the middle of the aisle, looking longingly at the frock while mumbling, shaking my head back and forth, and sighing to myself.

"I could wear it to a PTA meeting. No, a little over the top. I could wear it to a shower...if I actually had one coming up. Well, someone I know is *bound* to get married or knocked up! I really want to get it, but I don't work. I don't have a paycheck. Without a paycheck, I feel like

I need my husband's permission to buy this, since I am buying something for me and not the house or the kids. Wait! I take it back. I *do* work; I just don't have a paycheck. What's the going rate on a load of laundry? What type of premium is there on grocery shopping, cooking dinner, and running errands? No, still can't bring myself to do it."

So, I don't end up buying that dress. I turn, instead, to another dress just across the way. This one is equally as beautiful, yet a fraction of the cost. As I put my new purchase in the backseat of my car, I do not feel guilty. Don't get me wrong, Brad will still have sticker shock when the monthly Visa charges arrive, but there's one thing more important than using credit, and that is giving yourself credit where it is deserved.

∾ Diary Entry 85 ∾

The universe must have been aware of how much I had been smiling lately, because while eating my lunch today, the crown that I have had for almost a decade popped loose. It's not bad enough that the crown had to be on my front tooth, but underneath was a tooth that had been expertly crafted into a sharp point by my previous dentist. Yikes! I looked like I had just been cast as an extra in the film "Deliverance."

This is where I thanked my lucky stars that I didn't have a career as a broadcaster or some other public figure. Although I would not appear on TV in front of millions of viewers, it was just as imperative that the tooth be repaired so that it didn't appear that inbreeding was rampant in my family. The dentist squeezed me into his schedule and took molds for my new porcelain crowns. He gave me a temporary "tooth" that he said would hold me until the new set was complete. Call me conservative, but until I had my new, permanent choppers, this girl was not going to partake in eating corn or giving oral sex. Shoot, I should have had him write me a doctor's note!

∾ Diary Entry 86 ∾

After realizing how drastic a change a small tooth could have on one's appearance, I wanted to see what a different hairstyle could do. Over the years, I have tried a myriad of haircuts. They have ranged from having a "bob" to "The Farrah" and a brief stage where my hair was cut so short, people thought that I liked women. I would be much more adventurous with my hairstyle if my hair grew faster than a millimeter a decade.

But, today was the day. I went to see my hairstylist, Sonja, and told her that I was ready for something different. I wanted to take my typically wavy, nondescript hair and reinvent my look. So, she began what was a six-hour process of thermal reconditioning, otherwise known as "Japanese Hair Straightening." I left the salon with my straight locks blowing in the breeze. This is quite an accomplishment, since the humidity factor usually has it looking more like a Brillo pad and less like human hair.

I took my new hairstyle out for a spin and had mixed reviews. Some people commented that they loved it, and others remarked that I looked like a hippie from the '60s. Some said that it made me look ten years younger, and others said that I looked like I wanted to try out for "Pocahontas" at Disney World. But, for now, I like the change. I was slowly changing, so why not change my hair? I was experiencing a metamorphosis internally that I wanted to express externally. What was next, a tattoo?

∼ Diary Entry 87 ∼

Brad and I were at a holiday party, and in between eating brie and drinking eggnog, I saw a man approaching who looked very familiar. He wore a wide smile, and as he approached with his arm extended for a handshake or hug, I was searching my brain, straining to remember how I knew him.

"Hi, Rachel! How has life been treating you?" he asked. Well, that didn't give me much of a clue.

"Oh, it's treating me great," I replied. Was he a manager at Publix? Was he a father of one of the kids in Zach's class? Was he the attendant from Chuck E. Cheese's?

As I pondered the possible choices, he asked, "What have you been doing since leaving Merrill Lynch?" Bingo! He was a CPA that several clients of mine had utilized.

"Well, after leaving Merrill, I started a children's charity. Now, I am a stay-at-home mom," I declared.

"Well, that sounds nice," he added. After exchanging the obligatory pleasantries, I realized how much my life had changed in five short years. Besides the fact that my memory was failing and I couldn't recognize someone from a few years ago, I had created a new path for myself. It was a path that led me away from the buildings that hovered over downtown and toward white picket fences in suburbia. I put down my eggnog and opted for champagne. This new path I was following deserved a special toast.

"Here's to less stress and more fun," I silently toasted myself. Then I made a beeline to grab another Swedish meatball.

∿ Diary Entry 88 ∿

Snuggles has gone back and forth among Brad, Jessica, Zach, and me. There have been surprises of cars being washed, backs being rubbed, someone's chores being done for him or her, and the list goes on. It's nice to get a totally unexpected surprise that doesn't have to do with bubbles in the pool or my return address stamp being used to "brand" our leather couches. There definitely has been a conscious effort to be nicer to one another. We've been looking for opportunities to make the day special for someone else. I think the kids are beginning to realize that it feels just as nice to be the giver as it does to be on the receiving end. I just hope that they hold that thought as they encounter people outside our family.

∿ Diary Entry 89 ∿

This domestic thing is growing on me. Here I was, flitting around my kitchen, dressed in my dazzling green apron. If nobody knew better, I might have been mistaken for someone who enjoyed cooking. I was humming as I swung open cabinet drawers and grabbed the multitude of ingredients that were going to be part of my sumptuous dinner masterpiece. Just as I was emptying the flour into my KitchenAid, I realized that my hands were covered in gunk.

"Brad, can you grab me a spatula, please?" I asked. He dutifully went to the drawer to retrieve it but came back with a burger flipper.

"No! A spatula," I demanded.

"This is a spatula," he said incredulously.

"No, a spatula is a wooden stick with rubber at the top, which is used to swipe down the sides of the mixing bowl," I said impatiently.

"Mike," Brad said. "What am I holding in my hands?"

My brother casually glanced over and said, "A flipper."

"Isn't it called a spatula?" Brad continued.

"For the love of God!" I cried. "I know what a spatula is! Why are you arguing with me?" I yelled.

Now, not only am I not worthy of having an adult conversation concerning world events, I am getting challenged in my own domain? I should have home field advantage. I walked back to my bowl, shaking my head in disbelief and, for added effect, rolling my eyes in an overdramatic way. The subtlety was lost on him. Well, see if he gets second helpings of anything.

∿ Diary Entry 90 ∿

I can't seem to land the plane! I have never been so frustrated in my life. (Well, perhaps my first attempts at breast-feeding were a close second.) I get down to the runway, but it is more like a controlled crash than it is a landing. Until I master this skill, I can kiss getting a pilot's license goodbye. It's really something that I've dreamt of doing for years. I can't just abandon it now…can I? I have so much invested: time, money, and my ego. Buck up, lady, if you can make it through raising two children, you should be able to do anything! I'll just keep on repeating "I will be able to land…I will be able to land…I will be able to land" while my flight instructor, Bob, white knuckles it with me for the next hundred tries.

∿ Diary Entry 91 ∿

People used to say that I was "wound too tight." My type-A personality had been a boon in business, but it had sometimes been a detriment on the personal side of things. I wanted things done yesterday. I have always been a stickler for organization and schedules, and if you didn't have both in your life, well, then it spelled disaster. I lived by the mantra that the more you did in a day, the more productive a person you were. Being at home has definitely slowed down my pace from an all-out frenzied run to a brisk walk.

No longer am I sitting in traffic, with my hair perfectly coiffed, tapping my manicured nail impatiently against the steering wheel, calculating what route to take to make up for lost time. Instead, I find myself, on occasion, opting to take Jessica to school wearing my comfy pajamas! I reason that they look close enough to sweats, and if I am ever pulled over by an officer, my disheveled hair might convince the cop that I just got back from an intense run. (Of course, that wouldn't explain why I was wearing sandals and not cross-trainers.)

Not only have I ditched the business attire in exchange for my pj's, but I find myself being a more cordial driver. In traffic jams, I am not cursing under my breath, but I am actually motioning for cars who are trying to move lanes to cut in front of me. Red lights no longer make me mental; they are a welcome "time-out" to listen to a favorite song on my CD player. Road rage has evaporated, and in its place is a newfound bliss. Am I still wound too tight? Sure I am, but at least no bloodshed will be experienced due to traffic jams.

∽ Diary Entry 92 ∽

When I signed on to stay at home with the kids, little did I know that I was going to be keeping an eye on my mom as well. I think I have officially been indoctrinated into the "sandwich generation." This is where we not only have our children to care for, but we are now in a position to have to look after the well-being of our parents. Hopelessly sandwiched in the middle, hence the name. My dad passed away years ago, when Jessica was only two. Mom, while still leading a very active life at age 68, is in debatably good health and has a new boyfriend. Well, "new" if you don't count the last three times they have been together and broken up over the last year.

So, she tells me that she is going to sell her place, and they are going to move in together. "We're always together anyway, so, we figured, why have two homes?" she explained as nonchalantly as if she had just mentioned that she needed to pick up more orange juice from the store.

"That's a BIG deal," I said. "What if you break up again? Then where will you go?" I questioned, thinking in the back of my mind that my guest room might be where she would seek shelter.

"We don't plan on breaking up," she explained.

"Well, no one *plans* on breaking up. What about the breakups in the past? Did you plan those?" I asked. I was trapped in a weird time warp where my mom had morphed into a lovesick teenager, and I had become the responsible adult. I tried to think back to the sage advice she'd offered me during my teenage years. "Always wear clean underwear in case you are in a car accident" just didn't seem appropriate to say at the moment. Then, I realized there was no reasoning with me as a teenager. I was going to do what I wanted to do, because, by God, I knew what was best for me. And there I had it. She knew what was best for her. It wasn't easy to face, but I had to let her make her own choices.

"Well, as long as you are going to be happy, then, good luck with the move," I said protectively. She smiled and laughed a little. I am sure she was thinking that she wasn't asking for my permission but was simply informing me of her decision. I just hope that this decision is much sounder than my decision, as a teenager, to mix rum and beer and drink it through a funnel. Hopefully, the years of wisdom she has acquired will keep her living happily ever after…in some place other than "Chez Hamman."

∼ Diary Entry 93 ∼

I was at yet another birthday party for a kid in Zach's class. It's all a blur. How many times this year had I been bowling? How many times had I squeezed myself into a dwarfed race car at the Little 500? I can't remember what age is acceptable to drop your child and leave. I think I started to leave Jessica unattended at parties at the age of seven. But, then again, at six they seem so capable. Yeah, but boys don't seem as ready as the girls. The only thing they are "capable" of doing at this age is pulling the legs off of lizards and setting anthills on fire.

So, there I sat at Chuck E. Cheese's, dreading my next two hours in kiddie purgatory. I was pleasantly surprised by a new influx of parents—fresh meat in the parent circuit. As I sat there talking to a father named Robin, we covered traditional subjects like siblings; public schools versus private schools; and the litany of upcoming birthday parties.

Then, our conversation somehow drifted to hobbies, and Robin said that he was in the midst of making a movie. "Really? You're making a movie?" I said in what came out in an unintentional patronizing tone. I guess I was envisioning a grown man in his backyard, with his camcorder and homebuilt sets. "Have you ever made a movie before?" I continued.

He responded, "Yeah, a few years back, I made one with some of my buddies. You might have heard of it. 'The Blair Witch Project.'"

"That was you? I had no idea. It was excellent! It was one of the scariest movies I have ever seen!" I spit out the compliments at rapid speed in order to try and make up for my initial naivety.

Robin was very humble about his previous success and began to tell me about his new movie. He and his partners were in the pre-production phase of his new movie called "Altered" and were seeking investors.

"Investors you say?" I said with a gleam in my eye. Could I possibly have a different avenue in which to invest that would curb my day-trading habit? It was true. They were seeking investors to buy an equity share in their movie. As he told me the plot of his upcoming horror flick, a reverse alien abduction, I was intrigued. Could it be, a birthday party that led to something besides boredom coupled with a headache? Yes, Zach got to bond with his friends, while Mom got the details and requested a prospectus for a promising movie deal. It was the closest thing to discussing business that I had experienced in months. I could almost hear the wheels spinning in my head again as the dust and debris got brushed aside. Hollywood, here we come.

∼ Diary Entry 94 ∼

Our girls' weekend had finally arrived. Three days in paradise without children. Melissa and I met at the airport at the crack of dawn. From viewing my luggage, it looked like I had packed enough to stay two to three weeks. (Maybe wishful thinking that some snowstorm would have me trapped, unable to return to my domestic duties.)

Both of us had opted to wear jeans, boots, and the final touch of the West, cowboy hats. We were trying to set the mood for being in Montana, but I am fairly certain that we looked more like extras from "City Slickers" or "Urban Cowboy." We would have been better off just posting a neon sign on our foreheads that blinked "Tourist." It was okay by us, though—we are usually on the receiving end of tourists dressing badly. We get our fair share of hairy, bald, sunburned men, dressed in their black socks and sandals. It was our turn to look foolish. Besides, we would never see these people again.

Our friend Liz met us at the airport. Liz wore a wide grin. Either she was ecstatic to see us or she was busy thinking, "Hey, guys, remember, I do have to live here!" The first thing that we noted was that Liz's arm was in a sling.

"What happened to your arm?" I asked her.

"Just recovering from rotator cuff surgery. I'm doing great, just have to wear this thing for a few more weeks," she chirped.

"You should have told us that you were going to have surgery! We could have scheduled our trip for some other time," I told her.

"Don't be silly. I am fine. I just won't be joining you on the slopes," she answered. So, we took a very scenic drive into town and decided to eat lunch and look at the quaint boutiques, galleries, and shops that lined "downtown" Whitefish. On our way back to Liz's condo, we took a long, winding road past deer, frozen lakes, and pines that seemed like skyscrapers. Her place sat nestled at the base of the ski slopes.

We had successfully escaped the flat terrain and humid, 90-degree weather we had been experiencing in Florida. We both stood on her balcony overlooking a spectacular, panoramic view, which included the white-capped mountains of Glacier National Park. I felt like I had stepped into a postcard. After the tour of her digs, I decided to take a hot shower to wash the grime from my travels out of my hair. When I descended from my guest room with a towel perched on top of my head like Queen Nefertiti, I found Melissa standing over Liz who was slumped against the counter in her kitchen.

"Liz is having trouble breathing, and her side hurts," Melissa said in an alarmed tone.

"It's nothing," Liz said emphatically. But, as soon as the statement left her lips, another wave of pain shot through her, and she cringed.

"Let us take you to the hospital." She declined and swore that she must have just overdone the walking today and that she would return to normal once she lay down. This wasn't the case. As the pain persisted, we insisted that she phone a doctor. The doctor suggested that she keep an eye on her symptoms, and if they continued overnight, she should seek medical care in the morning.

We spent the night in, catching up, drinking wine, and wrapping our host in blankets and feeding her Tylenol. In the morning, Liz's symptoms had not magically disappeared but instead had worsened.

"Let us drive you to the hospital," we begged.

"No, I am going to see my usual doctor, and there is no reason for you to come with me," she explained. "Go hiking, go to the lodge and keep your appointments at the spa," she begged. "I am a big girl. I will be fine."

So, against our better judgment, she drove down the mountain alone. We embarked on our morning hike and felt guilty for not having accompanied her. After several drinks and a massage later, we called to check on her status.

"They found a pulmonary embolism. There is a clot in my artery, which leads to my lungs," she said grimly. "I need to be checked in to the hospital." We met her and drove her directly to the hospital. By now, it was nighttime, and she said she just wanted to get some sleep. She asked if we knew how to find our way back to her place, and we nodded in the affirmative even though we didn't have a clue.

Melissa and I stopped in town and had dinner, while Liz sat in a sterile hospital room eating what they claimed was Jell-O. We couldn't believe that her condition had turned out to be so serious. We finished dinner and laid off the alcohol, because neither of us felt confident maneuvering a strange vehicle up the snow-covered roads, even in a sober state. She was released the following day, armed with blood thinners and other medications. Her husband, David, flew in from Oregon, and we felt horrible that she had just had such a scare.

"I am so glad that you both were here with her," David said solemnly.

"So were we!" we said in unison. We spent the next day going off on our own to explore, while David and Liz stayed at their place. They apologized that it was no longer a "girls" weekend. Liz repeated again and again that she was so sorry that she ruined our trip. Sure, it was true. Neither of us had pictured our "carefree" weekend including hospital visits or medication runs on the itinerary. But, we couldn't bear to think of what might have happened if we had not pressured Liz to see a doctor. Life is so fragile and can turn on a dime. No, it wasn't the stress-free vacation we had envisioned; yet, we felt blessed that we had been there for a friend. Now, that is time well spent. It also served as a reminder of the role I play in my own family. I am there to tend for them. I am there to guide them. I am there to offer advice. I am there to offer comfort. I suddenly couldn't wait to return home.

∼ Diary Entry 95 ∼

After returning on the red-eye from Montana, there was nothing I would have liked to do more than to sleep the day away. No such luck. Today was Valentine's Day. Today was the day that I needed to show all the special people in my life that I loved them. Today, I was supposed to be organizing the Valentine's Day party for Zachary's class. When I'd volunteered for the assignment several weeks ago, I hadn't planned on a return flight to Orlando that arrived at midnight. I hadn't factored in that my car battery would be dead and that my new Audi would be stranded at Orlando International Airport. This meant I would not have my own car to tote cupcakes, juice boxes, and decorations to his class. I hadn't thought about the fact that with no sleep and no make-up, I would be very scary to the children in his class. (They might get confused and think we were celebrating Halloween again!)

But, in the name of St. Valentine, I rallied. I borrowed Brad's car; I made peanut butter and jelly sandwiches cut in the shape of hearts; I called the other mothers who were drafted for party duty to make sure that the kids would have a craft to bring home to their parents. The party went off without a hitch, mainly because six-year-olds do not have very high expectations. As long as sugar and candy are involved, they give it the big two thumbs up.

Next, I went home to wrap gifts for my family and to write cards declaring my passion, dedication, and undying love. Although I am sure that words were not properly strung together in the cards and that the packages I wrapped looked like they had been mauled by a pack of angry wolves, hopefully the sentiment was there. My biggest treat came when, after waiting for AAA for two long hours, I returned home to a homemade meal that Jessica had prepared, unsolicited. Brad and I usually spent Valentine's Day in a crowded restaurant, with an overpriced, preset menu coupled with bad service. Tonight, however, I was thrilled to be with the kids, celebrating together in our home.

∼ Diary Entry 96 ∼

I did my solo flight tonight! That's three takeoffs and three landings without another human being in the plane. Bob was hesitant to let me do it because the winds had been dicey, but they died down a bit toward sunset, to a level where he felt comfortable that I would not be a danger to myself or to the plane. He jumped out onto the taxiway and watched like a nervous mother as I positioned myself on the runway to take off. So, there I was, the plane, an amazing sunset, and me. I think I murmured something like "God, this is @*!#* incredible!" Fortunately, my mike was not keyed, so I spared the Sanford tower from hearing my expletive.

I had been practicing my landings for the previous two months, so I felt like I was ready. It was such a powerful feeling. I don't know what was more exhilarating—the sense of accomplishment or the sheer joy of being alone in the sky. When I successfully completed the third landing (successfully being a term I am using loosely...they weren't textbook landings, but I managed not to crash), we went into the operations center where Bob rang a bell and announced, "Rachel Hamman, just back from her first solo flight!"

Although there were only a dozen or so flyboys who gave the obligatory claps and whistles, I felt like I was on the red carpet about to accept an Academy Award. This was huge. It was really the first thing in my life I set out to do that was not work related. This was something that was mine and mine alone. This was something that I was doing for my own personal fulfillment. The fact that I had to work and study harder for this than anything else in my life also made the night that much sweeter.

To top the festivities off, I was then escorted to the flight prep room where Bob began the shirt-cutting ritual. He had warned me a few weeks back that when a pilot soloed for the first time, it was customary for the instructor to cut off the back of the student's shirt. I raised an eyebrow, thinking that I am so gullible, I'll be the first woman to let herself fall for the prank. But, after further inquiries, I was assured that both male and female students were part of the ritual. (My brother, Mike, cautioned me that if they tried to cut two nipple holes in the *front* of the shirt then maybe I am being had.) So, being forewarned, I had an extra T-shirt in my flight bag that I threw over the sweaty one I was wearing.

Bob began to cut, and I stood there with so many thoughts going through my mind. I was proud of myself. I was hungry. I was thinking that it had been a really long time since anybody had ripped, torn, or cut clothing off my body! It was one of my dreams to learn how to fly, and I was one step closer to making it a reality. After leaving the airport,

I met Brad, Jeff, and Beth to celebrate. Sure, I had a few glasses of champagne and a "Cosmo" or two, but nothing would compare to the natural high that I had just experienced at 1,000 feet above the earth. When it comes to dreams, the sky's not the limit…it's only the beginning.

～ Diary Entry 97 ～

I am 40 years old today. As I write the words, it still seems unlikely. How did the time sneak up on me? It seems like just yesterday that I was graduating from high school. The cruel reality is that Jessica will be doing so in just four short years. Four decades on this earth, and what have I done? Even though I consider myself to be an optimist, the perfectionist in me has never quite let me enjoy this day.

Brad always retells the story about the moment he knew he had fallen in love with me. It was several months after we met at Florida State University, and it was my 19th birthday. He had taken me to a fountain in the middle of the campus to drink some cheap champagne and throw pennies in to make a wish. (It's a good thing that pennies were traditional, because neither of us had more than a few red cents to our name.) I started sobbing and crying uncontrollably. He thought that I was a few drinks past my limit or that I had something horrible to reveal to him, like I had recently undergone a sex change. When he asked me what was wrong, through choked cries, I explained, "I haven't done anything worthwhile with my life. I haven't left my mark. I haven't done anything profound. I haven't found the cure for cancer!"

I think he spit out some champagne because he started laughing. "You are only nineteen!" he said to comfort me. "Nobody has found the cure for cancer," he continued. There was no consoling me. But, instead of thinking that my emotional outburst was neurotic, he found it endearing. And, the rest is history.

Now, here I sit, many years later, no longer crying on my birthday. Brad rented a big "Party Bus," and a dozen friends and I are traveling like rock stars. (Well, minus the piercings, the drugs, and the groupies.) As the music on the bus was blaring, people I love surrounded me. I was still reflecting on the mental scorecard of how I am contributing to society, but this is the first birthday that none of what I counted in my head had anything to do with the business world. My tick marks in the "win" column had to do with having made the choice to slow down long enough to access what I truly do want to do with the rest of my life. Still no cure for cancer, but I can safely say that the choices I make will have a positive effect on me. Conversely, they will also have a positive effect on the people who are in my life.

∾ Diary Entry 98 ∾

Ah, Spring Break. It's one of my favorite times of the year. I started a tradition seven years ago, when I was pregnant with Zachary, where Jessica and I would take a "Mommy/Daughter" trip. I wanted her to feel like she wasn't going to be replaced by the baby on the way. We could spend quality time together without her having to vie for my attention. (It was also a damn good excuse to plan an escape from the home front and from work.)

Over the years we have visited New York, Jamaica, St. Croix, San Francisco, the Bahamas, Sea Island, and Los Angeles. She has gotten to see more of the world in her 13 years than most people get to see in a lifetime. Well, this year, we had planned to take a cruise to Mexico. It all sounded innocent enough...sandy beaches, horseback riding, and Mayan ruins. Outdoor activities mixed with history; what more could we ask for?

The one thing that I forgot to take into account was that the last time we were on a cruise, Jessica was several years younger. In the meantime, puberty had hit, and now when she wore a bathing suit, there were packs of boys leering and drooling over her. I was all too aware how the waiter looked at her when he filled up her soda. I couldn't help but notice the heads turning to follow her when she walked by the edge of the pool. Jessica was unaware of the effect she had, but I knew I wasn't going to be able to sleep soundly until she was locked safely in our cabin at night.

Despite my new role as bodyguard, we did have fun on the ship. We lounged by the pool, ate tremendous amounts of food, shopped, explored, and took day trips in Cozumel. The biggest surprise came when we went to a "restaurant" for dinner called "Carlos and Charlie's." Sure, they served food, but this was *no* restaurant. I don't know if there is a drinking age in Mexico or not, but if there is, nobody enforces it. There were waiters and waitresses standing on tables, spraying tequila into the mouths of patrons sitting five feet away wrapped in butcher-block paper to catch the excess spray of alcohol. There was a shirtless man (with rock-hard abs, I might add) drinking what looked like an endless beer bong, while the rest of his party pounded on the table and rooted him on.

There was a conga line snaking through the restaurant, with kids under the age of 12 having rum poured in their mouths from the all too willing wait staff. It was like we had stumbled into a fraternity party. (This is from a girl who grew up in Ft. Lauderdale and who has witnessed her fair share of Spring Break activities.) Jessica was not part of the under-aged drinking train, but got quite an eyeful nonetheless.

After we ate our tacos, burritos, and chips, I thought it was best to leave. I thought to myself, "If this is what goes on before seven p.m., I don't want her to witness the erotic banana-eating contests and wet T-shirt contests that I'm certain are sure to follow." Brad would never forgive me. I take away our innocent teenager on a wholesome cruise and come back with a teenager requesting a pole be installed in her room so she can practice her bumping and grinding moves!

Back on ship, I packed my suitcase for the midnight roundup of luggage. I packed the tacky souvenirs I had bought for my family. How many shot glasses and pieces of bright painted pottery can one buy? Unbeknownst to me, Jessica was selecting a souvenir of her own. His name was Al! She had met a 15-year-old boy the last day of the cruise, and both of them were smitten. She was with a group of kids her own age, but I highly doubt that any of them were trustworthy chaperones. They exchanged a kiss, phone numbers, e-mail addresses and vowed eternal love.

When I told Brad about Al, he was relieved that the boy lived in Pittsburgh, Pennsylvania. He felt that a seven-state buffer was good enough. I was kind of hoping that it would be like a scene from "Titanic," where her shipboard beau was swallowed by waves, never to be seen again—only in the movies.

∼ Diary Entry 99 ∼

I haven't read Jessica's horoscope lately, but it must say something like "Good luck is in your ruling planet, so look forward to everything going your way!" Not only did she land a boyfriend on the cruise, but she had also gotten a call from an agent wanting to meet her.

We went straight from the Port of Tampa to an acting and modeling agency in the Tampa Bay area. We arrived at the agency a few minutes early. We sat in the waiting area surrounded by stark white walls and several black modular tables…very minimalist interior design. Either they had just moved, or they are getting ready to move out; or they are trying to impart an edgy feel. I hope it's the latter of the choices.

Jess looked bronzed and beautiful. Thanks to Pittsburgh boy, she also had a smile from ear to ear ever since we left the ship. She was called in to meet with the owner of the agency, and she walked back with confidence. (Or maybe she floated back, because she was still on cloud nine.) Several minutes elapsed, and just as I was thinking that I should go back to escort her to make sure she wasn't being introduced to the "casting couch," they called me in to join her. They went through a litany of questions to assess her experience and desire to become an actress.

When it was all said and done, they presented her with a contract. We thanked them profusely and took the contract with us to read before signing. After months of her sending headshots off with no reply, finally she could see a light at the end of the tunnel. She had taken the disappointment of being rejected and pressed on toward her goal. I had to admire her perseverance.

For being so young, she definitely has more maturity than some adults I know. We have always encouraged her to follow her dreams, and now she was one step closer to reaching them. There is nothing that compares with seeing your children accomplish what they set out to do. Hmmm, even more satisfying than, say, a business accomplishment? Maybe truly *being there* to witness times like these is why I have been having fewer withdrawal symptoms since leaving the workforce. I am a recovering workaholic who is slowly waking up to the joys I can find outside myself.

∼ Diary Entry 100 ∼

"Creepy" has been living it up. Over the last few months, he has been dressed in a variety of costumes for every occasion possible. At Christmastime, we dressed him in a red velvet cape, hat, and matching boots, and wrapped him in a festive box amongst the gifts we gave to Holly. Holly then dressed him in a tall chef's hat and a custom shirt made of red, white, and green fabric to set the tone for her Italian dinner. He was then "kidnapped" and tied to railroad tracks until Melissa's husband, Miro, sent Melissa to meet us at a day spa in exchange for Creepy's safe return.

Several weeks later, Melissa made a cute pair of chaps and a bandana for him to wear at their western-themed dinner party. A few weeks elapsed, and Holly had Creepy delivered to my house, nestled in a bouquet of gorgeous spring flowers to celebrate my solo flight. Lastly, Jodi dressed him up as a stripper for my 40th birthday. Creepy was wearing a diamond-studded G-string, a black blindfold, and bondage cuffs! (He apparently leads a more colorful sex life than I do!) Since the helium had long gone out of my birthday balloons, I figured it was time to "undress" Creepy and get him back to a pristine state. The G-string and blindfold came off without incident. However, when it came to the black electrical tape that was used for his cuffs, I was having some difficulty setting him free. I pulled a pair of scissors from the cabinet to help me pry off the tape.

I had one cuff off and three to go. I was working diligently on the second cuff when the scissors slipped, and the blade gouged into the "webbing" between my pointer finger and my thumb. Pain shot through my body like a spear, and blood began to spurt from my hand like a garden hose. Before I panicked, I decided to take a second look to see if the wound really matched the pain I was experiencing. After peering down into the half-inch gash and being able to see some ligaments, I felt that crying was warranted.

Luckily, my sister Shelly was in visiting from Colorado. She heard my cries for help and found me crouched in the kitchen with a bloody towel wrapped around my hand. After she and Jessica haphazardly dressed me, Shelly whisked me off to the closest hospital. There we waited in the emergency room for the doctor to come assess the damage.

"How did you do this?" the doctor asked as he cleaned away the blood with some chemical that burned like acid. Hmmm, how could I tell him that I was taking bondage clothes off my doll without sounding like a demented pervert? "I cut it with scissors," I answered honestly.

"What were you doing with the scissors that demanded such force?" he continued.

"I, err, I, uh, was opening up a present," I explained vaguely. He still wasn't buying my story. After getting several stitches and a plethora of medication for the pain, Shelly decided to share the truth with our good doctor. I think we sufficiently scared him off, because he never interfaced with us again. Instead, he sent an intern into the room to help us with the discharge procedure from the ER. So, Creepy has provided us with some good laughs, but like our parents used to say when we were kids, "It's all fun and games until someone gets hurt!"

∿ Diary Entry 101 ∿

Shelly's visit was coming to an end. I guess taking me to the hospital put her over her quota for fun. As a special send-off, I decided to cook a big brunch. And I do mean BIG. Since I had my hand wrapped in bandages all week, she had yet to witness my newly acquired cooking skills. I felt compelled to show off before she went back to Colorado thinking that I hadn't picked up any new tricks during my time as a stay-at-home mom. I would now dazzle her with my one-handed proficiency in the kitchen. I began mixing the batter for my fruit crepes. I then turned to my rolling pin to knead the dough for my cinnamon rolls made from scratch. Breakfast just wouldn't be breakfast without a hash brown and cheese casserole, so potato peels were flying. For the piece de resistance, I made a cornflake-encrusted baked French toast with honey-coated bacon.

As if that wasn't enough food to feed a third world country, Brad pitched in and made eggs hollandaise, accompanied by biscuits and gravy. It was a heart attack on a plate. I arranged all the food on our table, and it looked like it could go toe-to-toe with a brunch from a fine, five-star restaurant. As my mom, sisters, brother, Brad, and the kids stood over the sea of food, their mouths watered as they decided what to take first. They calculated what items would make the cut for their first round of food and what dishes would have to wait for their second or third helpings.

As all of us had food piled so high that it looked as if we were storing up to hibernate for winter, Zach stood at the table looking dejected. "What's the matter, honey? Do you want me to help you with your plate?" I asked.

"Where are the pancakes? I thought we were having pancakes!" he whined. With ten different dishes to choose from, the kid was still

searching for pancakes. I thought he would be thrilled that he was having something hot for breakfast and that, for once, he was not forced to
eat cereal like every other day of the month. There simply is no pleasing
everyone.

We talked, hummed, laughed, and ate before Shelly headed off to the
airport. At the end of the meal, we slumped on our couches and unbut-
toned our pants. I felt ill. I could feel my arteries hardening. Shelly left
anyway. She was not going to stick around to take me to my soon-to-
be-needed cardiologist visit!

∽ Diary Entry 102 ∽

It's bound to happen. No matter how much vitamin C we take or how
many echinacea we pop, when someone in the family gets sick, we *all* get
sick. The cold started a week ago with Jessica. I was the next lucky vic-
tim. I then passed the germs to Brad. Last but not least, Zachary was the
last to receive the cough, the runny nose, and pile of tissues balled up by
the side of his bed.

He was several days into the cold, and the symptoms seemed to gradually be getting better. He had already missed a few days of school, and
either he went back, or I was going to have to slit my wrists if I was
forced to watch another episode of SpongeBob SquarePants or Jimmy
Neutron.

As I was busy putting my makeup on, I said to Zach, "Since Daddy's
in the kitchen, can you ask him to get you a spoon for your medicine?"
He ran off to the kitchen, undaunted by his sniffles. When he returned,
no spoon was in sight.

"Where's the spoon for your medicine?" I questioned.

"I don't need a spoon. Daddy just gave me my medicine," he said
innocently.

"No, he couldn't have given you your medicine, because your cough
medicine is right here," I said as I pointed to the bright, cherry-red liquid. Brad strolled into the bathroom a few minutes later, and I asked,
"How could you have given Zach his medicine, when the medicine is
sitting right here?"

Brad looked momentarily confused and answered, "I gave him the
medicine that was in the kitchen."

"What medicine would that be?" I asked. We walked to the kitchen, and he motioned to the bottle on the counter. "That is NyQuil!" I yelled.

"So?" he said flatly.

"*Ny*Quil is called *Ny*Quil because it is for *night*time! It causes drowsiness," I continued.

"He'll be just fine. A little sleepy maybe, but he'll be okay," he assured me.

Sometimes, I feel like even the most simplistic tasks can't be executed unless I do them. Have I become so indispensable that if I don't get my child a spoon, he'll be drugged just prior to going to school? I suppose it could be worse. Brad could have given him the dog's flea medicine.

When I picked Zach up from school, I asked him if he had a good day. He whipped out his behavior chart to reveal all smiley faces. In recent days, the behavior chart had contained comments from his teacher, with notes such as:

"Zachary played with crayons instead of doing his math" or "Zachary fidgeted and could not sit still during circle time." Today, however, I found no additional notes, just Magic Marker smiley faces. Maybe Brad was onto something. NyQuil may be the next alternative to Ritalin.

∽ Diary Entry 103 ∽

One of the toughest things in my new position as a stay-at-home mom is that I feel like I am never in control. When I was in business, I at least had the *illusion* of being in control. I set the schedules; I determined the deadlines; I did the hiring; I outlined the goals and then implemented a plan that would take me there. At most times, I felt that I had a firm grasp of the reins.

Now, not only do I not have a grasp on the reins, someone has blindfolded me and has forced me to steer with my feet! There are days when the best made plans just evaporate into thin air. I can arrange to have the kids' portraits taken, and two days prior to the sitting, Zach gets the chicken pox. I can schedule a nice sit-down dinner together, but Jessica's play practice will run over; and instead of eating as a family, I am making macaroni and cheese for one child and then making grilled cheese for another two hours later.

I can do my best to plan activities for the kids that range from going bowling, to baking, to firing our own pottery, only to find my kids complaining that they are bored. I feel like Bozo the clown. Since when is it in a mother's job description to provide entertainment to our little ones 24 hours a day, seven days a week? Forget the flying lessons; I guess I should be taking a course in "Making Balloon Animals 101."

Just yesterday, I took Zach to a movie, followed by a trip to the park. I congratulated myself for what I believed to be the perfect combination. It was a main course of fun, with an order of fun on the side. When we returned home, after our five- hour outing, I went to my room to take off my sneakers, put down my purse, and wash my face. I couldn't have been gone for more than five minutes. When I walked into our family room, I bent over to pick up some magazines, which were thrown across the floor. As I stood up, something caught my eye. I stood there, head cocked, mouth agape, as I stared at the tic-tac-toe game that was carved into the leather on the couch.

"Zachary, what is this?" I yelled.

"X's and O's," he answered. I was not expecting the literal response.

"What did you do this with?" I moaned as I tried to wipe it off without success. "I used my fingernails," he replied.

"How many times do I have to tell you that we don't draw on furniture, or on the walls, or on our clothes, or on the pets!" I scolded.

"I'm sorry. I won't do it again," he pledged.

This is from the boy who, one year prior, used my return address stamp to "brand" the same leather couches. One only has to look closely to see "Rachel & Brad Hamman" stamped across the seat cushions. Now, when our company comes over, they will think that we are either overly possessive of our belongings, so much so that we have to label what is ours, or that we have given a whole new meaning to the saying "distressed leather."

As I shook my head and closed my eyes, I meditated. "Control. Maintain control." Maybe that was the lesson. Things are always going to happen that are out of my control. The only thing that I am capable of controlling is the way that I react to those things.

"Okay, God, lesson learned," I said out loud. I wanted to get this on the record before Zach is compelled to set the couches on fire.

∾ Diary Entry 104 ∾

Today, my baby girl turned 14. I spent the afternoon picking up her cake, getting assorted bags of junk food, and preparing for her party.

Jessica had invited seven girlfriends to her slumber party. This was her idea of fun. This was our idea of a very long, sleep-deprived night. Although I knew that the days of playing "Pin the Tail on the Donkey" were well behind her, she surprised me when she asked me a few weeks ago if we could rent a "Bouncy House" for her party.

"You mean the moonwalk things they have at fairs for toddlers?" I teased.

"Come on. You got one for Zach's birthday. They're fun!" she begged.

"You know if we get one, only two girls can go in at once. You aren't that little anymore," I reminded her.

"I know. Even with a few of us at a time, it will be a blast!" she implored.

So, there I was, ordering a bouncy house for my teenager. Being the detailed person that I am, I confirmed the delivery of the house both several days before her party and the day of. I was assured that the rental would be delivered before her friends arrived. We were now at "T minus one hour" until party time, and the inflatable house was nowhere in sight. After several calls to the rental company, a delivery truck showed up with the goods. It took the two delivery guys 20 minutes to erect the thing. (That's the longest time I've seen any man take to get something erected!)

By now, Jessica's friend Stephanie had showed up, and the two of them decided to be the first to christen the bouncy house. They were not out there for five minutes before they came inside. "Mom, the bouncy house doesn't work!" Jess complained.

"What do you mean it doesn't work?" I questioned.

"There's no bounce. We just sink into the plastic," Jessica elaborated. I went outside with them to demonstrate. Sure enough, they were sinking quicker than the stock market on Black Monday. I made a call to the rental company, and they promised to send out another unit. We waited for another half an hour, and the truck finally returned. The delivery guys, however, were empty-handed.

"Where's the new bouncy house?" I asked.

"We were told by the owner to pick this one up. We don't have any others we can bring," he said nonchalantly.

"I was promised that we would be sent another bouncy house that was not defective," I argued. I called the owner, who was not in the least bit interested that he had breached our contract. He was impolite, inflexible, and had evidently never taken a customer relations course in his life. I hung up the phone only after pledging to besmear his company's good name on the birthday party circuit! The doorbell began to chime, and Jessica's guests were arriving.

When I explained to Jess that she would not be getting another bouncy house delivered, she was upset. "What are we supposed to do for fun?" she asked.

"You can go swimming, watch movies, gossip about boys, make prank phone calls. You know, the usual slumber party stuff," I offered. She was clearly disappointed, and her eyes began to get glossy with tears. "Jess, you could use the money we were going to spend on the rental to take your friends to dinner on a different night. Or, you and Stephanie could go get manicures and facials next weekend," I said.

"That doesn't help me with something fun to do tonight," she replied. If she had been bratty about it, I would not have taken pity on her, but she wasn't. Although Jessica has never wanted for anything, I don't consider her spoiled. She is grateful for what she gets, and she buys much of her own clothes and entertainment with money she earns from baby-sitting neighbor kids. She wasn't stomping her feet or throwing a tantrum like the wretched little girl from "Willie Wonka and the Chocolate Factory" who screamed, "I want the goose that lays the golden eggs, Daddy!" She was simply disappointed.

I grabbed our yellow pages and began to brainstorm. Who could I call on short notice to fill our bouncy house void? I flipped the phone book open to "Parties and Events." Clowns? No. Face painters? No. Strippers? Definitely, no! Then, I stumbled on an ad for a psychic who did parties, weddings, conventions, and Bar Mitzvahs.

I caught "Madam Natasha" on her night off. When she answered the phone, I asked, "Do you ever book engagements on short notice?"

"How short of notice?" she responded.

"Is one or two hours notice out of the question?" I asked with trepidation. She agreed to come. Either she could hear the desperation in my voice, or she needed to earn some extra cash for a new crystal ball. She then informed me that she could do a variety of things with the girls. She had her traditional readings utilizing tarot cards; she could do handwriting analysis; she could read palms; and she was a certified belly dance instructor. I asked her to leave the belly dancing gear behind. I was already wondering how some of the parents might react to having their children exposed to a psychic. In addition, I didn't want to have to explain why their daughters had learned to thrust and gyrate, with thimbles on their fingers, while simultaneously doing a backbend. (I could save those lessons for me and *my* girlfriends!)

She arrived as promised, right on time. I had not told Jessica that she was coming, in case she experienced car trouble. I didn't want to have a second disappointment that evening. Madam Natasha arrived, dressed in full gypsy regalia and a sack full of her "trade tools." The girls were intrigued and mesmerized by the colorfully dressed woman in our foyer. I decided to crash the party and sit in on this portion of the evening, just in case parents had any questions about what they were exposed to. (I didn't want any rumors going home that they were forced to drink goat's blood, or that a pentagon was painted on the Hammans' floor.)

Madam Natasha stayed the next two hours, entertaining the girls with glimpses into their futures. All of it was very generic but positively spun advice. (Sort of like having Oprah dressed in costume.) Jessica came up to me after the psychic had left and thanked me for making the extra effort to find her and convince her to come. She said she and her friends thought it was so cool. So, I was pleased at tonight's outcome. I was glad that Madam Natasha stepped in to solve our bouncy house dilemma. (Although, I have yet to see if we will experience any backlash from having a politically incorrect party performer.) I was happy that the girls had fun. I was proud that Jessica was growing up to be such a level-headed, gracious, and loving young woman. I was ecstatic that we still have a few more years until her birthdays become a co-ed event!

∾ Diary Entry 105 ∾

A note came home from school last week announcing "Pet Day" in Zachary's class. The fact that our home has been turned into a place that Dr. Doolittle would have been proud to call his own made Zach's selection process a difficult one.

"Should I bring Nala?" he pondered. "No, she doesn't do any tricks," he sighed. "Oh, Abbey!" he squealed. "Nah, she won't let my friends hold her," he thought out loud. "How about my two turtles?" he said while feeling his chin, as if he was stroking a goatee. I shot that one down quickly. I was not going to be known as the mom who spread the salmonella epidemic through the entire kindergarten population.

By process of elimination, he chose our dog Josie as the lucky show-and-tell prop. Pet Day had arrived, and I was to meet Zachary in his homeroom class, with dog in hand. Jessica had given her a bath the night before, but she had escaped this morning into a nearby pasture and returned with knotted fur and burrs stuck to her paws. I tried to re-beautify her as best as I could before her big debut. I fastened her leash around her neck and grabbed her favorite ball and a few dog treats that I planned to use as enticements. I dragged her into the car where she promptly began to quiver and shake. I tried to console her, but she was sure that I was driving her to the V-E-T. I guess I would be scared, too, if I thought I was on my way to get multiple shots or a thermometer shoved up my ass.

Once on campus, I thought she would calm down, but she was still acting skittish. Random children were running at her on the sidewalks, wanting to touch her. In Josie's brief life of three years, the only experience she has had with children has been Zachary lying on her, squeezing her, or attempting to ride her; so, I had to warn the kids that she was "feeling shy" right now. I didn't want Zachary's Pet Day to resemble a scene from the movie "Cujo."

We made it to Zach's classroom without incident. (That's if you don't count Josie taking a crap on the nicely manicured greens of the campus as an incident.) We were greeted by Zach's teacher, who got the kids to sit in an orderly fashion. Zach stood at the head of the class, with a choke-hold on Josie, and proudly announced, "This is my dog!"

"What is the dog's name?" Mrs. Parkins questioned.

"Josie," Zach responded.

"Is Josie a boy or a girl?" Mrs. Parkins asked.

"Josie is a girl, and she can do lots of tricks!" he added. He began by showing his classmates how Josie could sit on command, lie down, and roll over. He then showed them how Josie could catch the ball in midair and retrieve it promptly. Everyone in the class wanted a turn. Ten treats later, I figured that although Josie would love to play catch all day, if she was given any more treats, she would need to have another "incident" in Mrs. Parkins' class.

"Very impressive, Zachary," Mrs. Parkins cheered. "By the way, what type of dog is she?" she asked.

"She is a Yellow Leopard!" Zachary answered.

"Close, honey. She is an Australian shepherd," I corrected him.

"Oh, those are very smart dogs," Mrs. Parkins provided.

"Yeah, I guess," Zachary said. "But, she can't be that smart if she goes poop on our rugs at home almost every day."

"Interesting tidbit," Mrs. Parkins said, trying to stifle her laughter. Now, it was my turn to "play dead." Just another example of how staying at home is a humbling experience. I could teach thousands of children to volunteer and to help others in the community, but I couldn't teach my dog to stop shitting on our carpet.

∽ Diary Entry 106 ∽

I was driving Jessica to school today, and while channel surfing on the radio, I heard the announcer declare, "Today is Take Your Daughter To Work Day." My heart immediately sank. This was the first time in six years that Jessica would not be accompanying me to my job. I remember her helping with copies at the ripe age of eight. She helped to do mailings at ages nine and ten. When she was 11, she would assist in preparing goodie bags for some of our community service projects. By ages 12 and 13, she was answering phones, running errands, and preparing flyers for upcoming fund-raising events.

Today, however, was a different story. "Didn't you want to go to work with Dad?" I asked her.

"No, it's boring there," she answered.

"You would rather go to school than get some real-world experience?" I probed.

"Pretty much," she said flatly.

"So, I guess that means you don't want to go to work with me this year?" I questioned.

"You don't work anymore, remember?" she said sarcastically.

"I do too work!" I said emphatically. "I just don't get paid for what I do!" I said, shaking my head. I suppose that it would not be a thrill for her to watch me do laundry. Nor would it be a high point in her day to escort me to the grocery store to gaze with bated breath while I crossed off items, one by one, from my list. Had I lost the respect of my daughter? Did she see me as a noncontributing member of society? Was she too young to remember my former life and all the things I had accomplished in a male-dominated world?

Just as I was beginning to wallow in my self-doubt and pity, we pulled up to school. As she got out of the car, she stuck her head back in and said, "Don't sweat it, Mom. I already know what the best mom in the world does during the day. I love you." As I drove off, I could feel the tears rolling down my face. She just confirmed that the best thing I can do for her is to show her who I am and what I stand for every day of the year instead of what I do for a career on one given day.

∽ Diary Entry 107 ∽

The end of baseball season has arrived. Well, really the end of "T-ball" season to be exact. There is an important distinction to be made between the two. The distinction is that as a parent of a "T-ball" player, you log approximately one and a half hours less time sitting on the bleachers per game. We went from a league where they pitched to the kids, to a league where the kids hit the ball off the "T."

Although the kids may have learned hand-eye coordination with being pitched to, the games felt like they lasted an eternity. This new league was organized and ran like clockwork. Yet, even with the shorter play time, I was happy to see the season coming to an end. We packed up the car and drove to a local park for the celebration. Brad was surprised when Jessica agreed to come with us to the awards ceremony. I knew better. She was lured there with the promise of pizza and the potential of catching glimpses of cute teenage boys who played in the high school league.

The coach called each of the boys forward and presented them with their own bobble-head trophy. Zach was so excited. "Look! It has my name engraved on it!" he hollered, as the metal head of the trophy bobbed up and down. Brad and I gave each other a knowing glance and began a side bet as to how long the trophy would be in one piece.

Forty-five minutes after we returned home, Zach came downstairs from his room with the bobble head in one hand and the arms of the statue in the other. It looked like I would be going to our local trophy store to find a replacement. It also looked like Brad owed me a back rub.

I had predicted that the trophy would not stay in its current state for over an hour. As a mom, you learn to turn tragedy into something positive.

∽ Diary Entry 108 ∽

I yawned and stretched like a cat, basking in the sun as the light came streaming in our bedroom windows. It looked like a picture-perfect day. That was until a fully dressed Brad bent over to kiss my head as he was leaving for work and said, "I wish I could lie in bed all day with you." I was momentarily quiet as I reeled from the comment.

"I don't lie in bed all day!" I retorted. "Zach wakes up in another five minutes, and then it's time for me to get him ready for camp. After I clean up the Fruity Pebbles that he has spilled all over the table and floor, it's time to argue with him that he may not wear his Batman costume to soccer practice. When he has relinquished his cape, I then have to pull him away from his cartoons long enough to brush his teeth and hair. There is a second change of clothes after there is more Crest toothpaste on his shirt than he gets into his mouth. After I shuttle him off to his 'half day' camp (I don't know in what culture a half day is equivalent to two and a half hours!), the 'break' I experience is filled with errands like fixing the taps on Jessica's shoes; having Zach's team picture framed; or waiting on the pest control guy so that I am not greeted by a spider the size of my hand the next time I venture into the bathroom. Mom's taxi service then departs to pick up Zachary and bring him home for lunch. Since we do not have a butler at our beck and call, that would make me the cook and cleanup crew. By this time, Jessica is off to her play practice. Since she cannot drive herself, I again load Zachary into the car, and we drive to the other side of town so that someday Jessica can see her name in lights on Broadway. Then, I do fun things like pick up flowers for our yard and, if I'm lucky, a trip to the vet with one of our three pets. There is just enough time to cook dinner before it's time for me to hop back in my car to pick up Jessica. So, I don't appreciate the fact that you think I get to lie in bed all day and watch TV, eating bonbons!"

Brad looked confused, and his eyes darted back and forth. I was not certain if he was rattled from my speech or if he was surveying the bed to make sure that I didn't have any sharp objects nearby, ready to pull a Lorena Bobbitt.

"I don't think that you get to lie in bed all day," he quickly explained. "I know you are busy and have things to do. I was just thinking how great it would be if both of us could just rest here all day, holding each other, with no responsibilities," he said in a sullen tone.

"Well, it didn't sound that way to me," I said defensively. He gave me a reassuring hug and then left for work. The purring kitten had just transformed into a tigress that, instead of protecting her young, was protecting her territory. Had I overreacted? Had I become so sensitive about my new role as a housewife that I felt threatened if anyone hinted that I was doing less than my share?

Just then, Zach came bounding onto the bed. My five minutes of free time had been squandered on useless, verbal combat. Damn.

∿ Diary Entry 109 ∿

When I was little, my brother and I would go to camp for the summer in Hendersonville, North Carolina. From the time I was in fifth grade until I was in eighth grade, Mike and I would be gone for six weeks straight. Camp Highlander was amazing. We got to experience horseback riding, water-skiing, rappelling mountains, hiking, shooting rifles, river rafting, archery, hayrides, and eating s'mores by the light of the campfire. We thought it was the greatest time on earth, but we thought our parents must have been even more elated to have the house to themselves while we were gone.

So, why wasn't I happy that I was putting Jessica on a plane to go to Chicago for one measly week? Uncle Corky had given her the trip as her graduation gift from eighth grade. (It must be a northern thing, because I was not planning on getting her anything besides a card and her choice of where to go to dinner to commemorate her moving on to high school.) We had been away from both kids when we had taken business trips or extended trips out of the country. This, however, was different. This would be her first time visiting her cousins without our supervision. It's not that I envision her drinking in bars on Rush Street or that she will return to us with a belly button ring. I just worry that she'll be safe.

So, as I walked her to her departure gate, I gave her the rundown. "Make sure to have your cell phone charged," I said. "Oh, and when you are out, make sure you are always with someone. Strangers typically won't abduct a pair of girls," I reminded. "Don't talk to anyone who is old enough to have facial hair," I threw in for good measure.

"Mommmmmmm. I am not a baby. I know what to do," she chided.

"I know you're not a baby. That's what I am afraid of!" I answered.

I remember putting her on a plane to meet my mom when she was nine. At the time, the airlines gave her a big sticker to affix to her chest that read "Minor." I wish I had one of those stickers now to warn all the perverts out there that they are staring at jail time if they mess with her. I sat with her at the gate until I had to leave to get Zachary. I hugged her for the hundredth time, and she assured me that she was going to be fine.

I walked down the corridor of the airport and couldn't help myself. I turned around, one last time, to sneak a peek at her. There she was, putting her iPod into her ears. I walked back toward her, and she looked at me puzzled.

"What's the matter?" she asked.

"You need to take off the iPod in order to hear the announcements that they make about flight delays and gate changes!" I told her.

"I was just planning to watch when everyone else gets up to board the plane," she explained.

"Humor me. Take the headphones off until you are in the air," I insisted. She relented, and I gave her another parting kiss. Just when I was feeling like I might be a tad too cautious, I suddenly felt that rafting a class-four rapid was safer than letting her travel alone.

∾ Diary Entry 110 ∾

It seems that the pattern Jessica established of trying a multitude of activities before she settled on one has been passed down to Zach. He has gone from karate, to T-ball, to trying his hand at acting. I suppose he was only curious what his big sister does inside the structure that we drive her to ten times per week. He asked us to sign him up for a course called "The Magic Story Box." The paragraph that explained what the kids would be engaged in described things like "Imaginative Play," "Character Development," "Staging and Placement." The parents were promised that by week's end, the kids would have a performance to showcase their talents.

I arrived at the theater early to ensure that I would get a seat up front and center. (One perk of being a stay-at-home mom was that I was punctual because I was not waylaid by a conference call or a meeting that ran late.) The first play they performed was "Little Red Riding Hood." This rendition was done with a dozen five- and six-year-olds who were being coached to remember their lines by a very patient teacher/narrator.

Zachary played "The Big Bad Wolf." My chest swelled with pride that my kid had secured one of the leads. Just as I was thinking that the theatrical gene must run in the family, I was brought down a few pegs when Zach then played "a bed" in "Goldilocks and the Three Bears," followed by him starring as "one side of the brick house" in "The Three Little Pigs." So much for him joining his sister on the silver screen. Truth be told, he was as cute as could be in all three acts. I was just happy that I was able to have the luxury of time to come to watch him. How many other instances in his life am I going to get to utter the words, "You were the best brick wall I have ever seen!"

∿ Diary Entry 111 ∿

My day started by showering with two men. Granted, the men were only ten inches tall and were made out of plastic, but Aquaman and Spiderman added a little extra something to my morning scrub. Zachary is forever leaving an arsenal of toys in our bathroom, and these were this morning's shower guests. I was thinking that my day would be uneventful, but the miniature plastic tines from Aquaman's spear that had lodged between my toes should have been a hint that it would be anything but normal.

For the last several days, we had been working with Zach to teach him to ride his bike. Two years ago, when Zach was four, "Santa" brought him a bike. Santa's helper had apparently not done her measuring correctly and had picked out a bike that was several inches too big for young Zach. After several tumbles off the bike, it was another two years before he climbed back on the proverbial horse. (This was only after Zach had several play dates with girls where they rode past him on their pink Barbie bikes with purple and silver fringe flying from their handlebars in the breeze. Seeing his female friends passing him with ease didn't sit well with my competitive boy.)

So, after weeks of aborted attempts, he was at the point where he was finding his balance. He could ride straight down the road for 100–200 yards without hitting a curb, a tree, or the neighbor's cat. Stopping and turning were an entirely different story. Just as I thought he had the whole agility and balance thing licked, he fell off his bike, and with blood streaming down his arms and legs, he vowed that he would never ride again.

"Never" lasted 45 minutes when Brad solved the dilemma by going to Toys "R" Us and buying a bike that fit him properly. With the smaller bike, Zach found his confidence. In no time flat, he was turning, braking, and looking like he owned the road. So, today when he asked to ride again, I was eager to oblige. Out we went into the blistering Florida heat. I helped secure his helmet and gave him a slight push to get started. He did fine for the first five seconds, and then he became wobbly and launched himself, face first, into the pavement.

He stood up, shrieking, and blood was flowing from his mouth. "My teeth!" he cried. The ruby red liquid was not allowing me to see if he had damaged any teeth. "They are pushed up into my gums!" he hollered. We came in and washed off the blood, and I immediately called our dentist. X-rays revealed that he had not damaged the bridge or the permanent teeth. I breathed a sigh of relief.

When we returned home, I made him a chocolate shake for lunch. (Ice cream helps to ease the pain and doesn't require intensive chewing.) I left the kitchen to talk with Jessica in the den, and not three minutes went by before he came in with his hand gushing with blood.

"What happened?" I cried, jumping from my chair.

"The tip of my finger came off!" he groaned. Two days ago, he had sliced the top of his finger with a pair of kids' safety scissors. Safety scissors…go figure! The cut was not deep enough to warrant stitches, but it left a horseshoe-shaped flap of skin on the tip of his pointer finger. The flap reopened yesterday, when Zach and I were playing Putt-Putt golf. Zach was climbing on some rocks and slipped into the mucky, sludge-ridden waters of the "Congo Golf River." I was horrified when I saw the dirty water he had fallen into with his multiple open wounds. It was a staph infection waiting to happen. After the 18th hole, I took him home and put him in a piping hot shower and continued the germ holocaust by dousing him with enough hydrogen peroxide and Neosporin to treat an entire hospital ward.

So, apparently, after today's bike accident (or something sharp that Zach encountered while drinking his milkshake), the finger had ruptured again. Blood was everywhere. It looked like I had stepped into a scene from "The Texas Chainsaw Massacre."

"I can't handle any more blood or any more injuries," I thought to myself. I took out the first-aid kit from the cabinet for the third time in two days. Jessica then helped me mop up the trail of blood leading from the kitchen to our master bedroom. When Brad came home, I looked as stressed as I felt. It seemed as if I had just worked a ten-hour shift as a doctor in a busy emergency room.

"You wouldn't believe my day," I whined. I gave him a blow-by-blow description of the dental trauma and the bloody scene that followed. After I finished venting about the day, I returned to the warmth of my shower (sans the action heroes). As I reflected on the events of the day, I was struck by a thought. Yes, it was far from how I wanted the day to unfold. I would have preferred that Zach hadn't injured himself…twice. I would have preferred that blood had not been strewn across my counters and hardwood floors. I would have preferred that it be a day filled with fond memories of me watching my son ride his bike. I would have preferred to be giving him kisses and treating him to a Popsicle versus giving him gauze and antiseptic.

The thought that did make me feel good, however, was that I had been there for him. I was glad that it had been me and not a daycare worker who scooped him up and ran with him to survey his wounds. I was glad that it had been me who accompanied him to the dentist instead of a relative. I was glad that it had been me who comforted him while he was in pain. As stressful as the day was, I was grateful that I could be there for him, just as he would be by my side tomorrow when we went shopping to restock our first-aid supplies.

∾ Diary Entry 112 ∾

Today was a big day for me. I was scheduled to take the FAA written exam for my private pilot's license. I have been studying like a fiend (in between play dates, bathroom breaks, or after everyone was asleep). Several nights ago, I was busy cramming several textbooks worth of knowledge into my already cluttered brain and felt like I was just spinning my wheels. Had college been so long ago that I had lost my ability to study? Or, was it the fact that I had absolutely no other responsibilities while I was in college that allowed me to focus with razor sharp precision?

Brad teased me and asked, "Why are you so stressed about passing the exam? It's not like you'll lose your job if you don't pass. Don't they allow you to take it more than once? Plus, don't you only have to get a seventy percent to pass? You can do that in your sleep," he assured me.

"Yes, I can take it again, but I don't want to have to! It's an ego thing. If I study hard enough, I should be able to pass. Plus, if I only get a seventy percent, that means that while I'm actually up in the air, the other thirty percent that I got wrong might just be what I need to know to save my life!" I explained. Well, pass I did. When I punched the button in the testing lab, the one that asked if I was "Ready To Score?" I was shocked when a 93 percent came flashing on the screen. Was it my score, or had I inadvertently grabbed the score of the book-smart, 22-year-old-looking kid sitting next to me? No, the test proctor assured me that I had, indeed, passed the test.

I walked out of there feeling great. The written test was behind me, and I had practically aced it. I had always been an A student, but it had literally been decades since I had to prove that I still had it. On my drive home, I was feeling pretty good about myself.

"Ninety-three percent!" I repeated as I gave myself an "at a girl" glance in the rearview mirror. That means I only missed four questions. "Not too shabby for an old broad," I thought giddily. I called Brad at work and told him the good news. "I scored a ninety-three percent!" I said proudly.

"That's great. I knew you'd do well," he congratulated me.

I hung up and sighed a deep breath of relief. The written test was over. Now, I'll keep my fingers crossed that the four questions I did not get right never come back to haunt me!

∼ Diary Entry 113 ∼

It's Labor Day and we had friends and family over for a barbeque. Mom and Larry came, too, and they watched as we played several highly competitive games of water volleyball. We gorged ourselves on chips, beer, brownies, and hamburgers. We not only didn't wait the recommended 20 minutes prior to going swimming, we ate while we were swimming.

Shortly after the meat from the grill had been devoured, I sat with my mom and munched on the toffee squares she had brought. Somewhere in the conversation, my mom said, "Hey! Did I tell you what Michael gave Larry and me as a housewarming gift?"

"No, what did he give you?" I asked nonchalantly.

"He gave us the trip for two to Ireland that he bought at the gala!" she squealed with delight. She was like a little kid who had just been given a year's supply of candy. "We are planning to go in the fall! Isn't that exciting?" she beamed. I started to laugh uncontrollably.

"What's the matter? What's so funny?" she said. I excused myself from the table and went into the laundry room to retrieve a wrapped package, no bigger than a bread box. "What's this for?" she asked.

"It's your housewarming gift from me and Brad," I managed to get out between laughs. She tore open the bright pink wrapping to reveal a bag of mocha-scented potpourri. "Michael gets you a dream vacation overseas, and we get you flavored wood chips! Suffice it to say, I'd be utterly embarrassed right now if you hadn't raised us repeating the mantra 'It's the thought that counts!'"

∾ Diary Entry 114 ∾

I did the unthinkable today. I attempted to do back-to-school shopping with Zachary in tow. Usually, I'll get his things during a few hours of power shopping on the weekend so I don't have to go through the hassle of hearing, "I don't like that!" "This is too big!" "That's ugly!"

But, today, I had a momentary lapse in judgment and took him along. After he played hide-and-go-seek in the racks of clothes and nearly gave me a heart attack because I thought he had been kidnapped, he went crawling across the floor, collecting dozens of discarded pins. (Note to self: Feeding your child a large ice cream cone, dipped in chocolate sprinkles, prior to wanting him to behave is setting yourself up for failure. Not only have you given away your dangling carrot tool, but you have unwittingly given your child enough sugar to keep him buzzing for hours.)

As we exited the store, I remembered that I was out of my blush and concealer, and I made a pit stop at the makeup counter. As I wearily approached the counter, hands full of bags, a woman dressed in business attire darted in front of me.

"I'm on my lunch break. I have to rush to get to a meeting!" she stated curtly. I stared her down but did not answer as I watched Zach hopping around me in circles, pretending he was a frog.

I felt like responding, "Oh, no rush here! I just have a six-year-old whom I have spent the last sixty minutes trying to corral. How could you understand that it has taken the strength of ten men to keep his grimy little fingers off of all the clothes so that I don't end up having to purchase a cashmere sweater laden with bubble gum? How could you possibly understand that I don't have an endless amount of time? Just because I am not working in an office, it doesn't mean that I don't have a schedule to keep. In twenty minutes, I have to pick my daughter up from her acting class. After that, I have to take both of my kids for eye appointments to see if they'll need glasses for school. Following that, I have to meet the exterminator at my house so that I don't find bugs the size of small pack animals in my garage! No schedule for me to keep! But, by all means, you go right ahead!"

That's what I would have said if I hadn't noticed that she was not wearing a wedding ring. That's what I would have said if I hadn't noticed that her nails were perfectly manicured and that her designer suit was perfectly pressed. All three signs led me to the conclusion that she was not a stay-at-home mom.

Only another stay-at-home mom could empathize with the demands that seemed invisible to the rest of the world. Only a stay-at-home mom could commiserate with the stresses, both financial and emotional, that we encounter on a daily basis. That's when it hit me. How many other women are going through the same trials and tribulations? How many other women have decided to trade in their briefcases for diaper bags? There must be throngs of women who have made the same life choices. Why then is it that you don't hear about them? Why is it that you can find support groups for every minor disease known to man, but you rarely find support for one of the largest and most rapidly growing conditions known to women…being a stay-at-home mom. I was now on a mission to find other successful women and hear what they were experiencing after they chose to derail their careers in the pursuit of raising their families.

∼ Diary Entry 115 ∼

The quest for what stay-at-home moms had to say about their chosen path had begun. I used a variety of methods to seek out women who had left powerful positions and lucrative careers to be home with their children. I began with the obvious and e-mailed friends who had made the decision to leave their respective careers to be full-time caregivers. These friends were intrigued by my request for them to write down their emotions about becoming a stay-at-home mom. Some shot off short stories right away.

Others felt that they were too busy with their daily activities to find time to write down their thoughts. Still others said they had plenty to say, but if they wrote down their true thoughts on the matter, they would have to change their names to fend off potential divorce proceedings! I then placed ads in several local newspapers and school circulars. This coupled with ads I posted on stay-at-home mom-related Web sites and an ad in a national parenting magazine should do the trick.

∼ Diary Entry 116 ∼

The stories have been pouring in. The women who responded to my ads seemed quite thrilled to have an outlet to discuss how being a stay-at-home mom compares to their former lives as bustling professionals. These women were anxious to share their emotions. It was almost as if they had never been asked the question. Maybe they had been asked the question before, but this time, they had been asked to share the truth about how they are dealing with their life shift.

Some stories were funny. Some stories were touching. Some stories spoke of loss of identity, while others talked of new strengths found. I was amazed at each story I read. These women were me, and I was them. Although each of them had their own spin and their own tonality about the transition they had made to become a stay-at-home mom, there was a commonality that remained. Many of the women who wrote mentioned how cathartic it was to express the myriad of feelings that you go through when you leave a structured career for the chaotic yet wonderful profession of motherhood. Let the "group therapy" begin!

PART II

GROUP THERAPY

CHAPTER 4

FROM BREADWINNER TO FIXING DINNER

∽ I Used to Wear Prada *by Lora Crone* ∽

I stopped working as a national sales manager for a corporate sporting goods company six years ago. It was a wonderful career. I utilized my business skills, met lots of interesting people, and thought I contributed to the world. I was organized and had lots of time on my hands. On rare occasions, I would get up at 5:30 a.m. to catch a flight or to work out.

Now at 5:30 a.m., I'm frantically making breakfast and school lunches. (I'm just waiting for the day my children take bacon and eggs to school and eat a turkey sandwich and carrots for breakfast.) During this morning's routine, I pondered that cliché, "Before children, what did I do with all of my free time?" Since my brain cells are a bit foggy from either lack of sleep or years of inhaling dirty diaper odors, I'm not sure my life before children was as wonderful as I thought it was.

I used to:

- Watch a TV show uninterrupted.
- Drive a clean sports car.
- Sleep. Period. No interruptions. No one breathing in my face or tapping me on the shoulder with stuffed animals in tow at 3:30 in the morning.
- Eat a warm meal.
- Stress over a broken nail or not getting in for a pedicure.
- Drink a bottle of wine and not worry about the ramifications of the next day.

- Read intellectually stimulating books.
- Have a sterile and organized house.
- Listen to music I wanted at any volume.
- Work. Work. Work.
- Call girlfriends and talk about our next social outing.
- Stay out until the aforementioned 5:30 a.m.
- Shop for cute clothes—in the couture section.
- Tell my husband I loved him as I was running out the door.

While putting the finishing touches on the lunches, and after getting the kids to actually sit and eat their breakfast, I then thought, "Were those things really so important?" Nobody told me (or reminds me) how wonderful children could be.

Now I get to:

- Receive hugs and kisses in the morning, after-school, and before bed.
- Hear "Thank you, Mommy" for a quick diversion into McDonald's when broccoli is on the dinner menu.
- Have pillow fights with LOTS of giggling.
- Play the tooth fairy at midnight.
- Know Dick, Jane, Spot, Puff, and Baby very well.
- Sing every Disney song known to mankind at the top of my lungs.
- Learn all of the names of the Thomas Train engines and Polly Pocket dolls.
- Get sick from jumping on the trampoline.
- Stress over my child's broken heart.
- Familiarize myself with every Barbie and which doll belongs to which outfit. (By the way, this is harder than figuring the gross margin return on investment for 500 items for ten customers.)
- Call my daughters' friends' parents (who are now dear friends) to talk about our kids' next social outing or current crisis.
- Manage to stay up until nine p.m.
- Shop for cute clothes—in the kid's section.
- Thank my husband every day for a wonderful life and tell him how much I love him as we watch our beautiful daughters blossom into young ladies.

Things I've learned:

- It's more difficult to schedule a play date than to get an appointment with the president of Nordstrom.
- Always buy a new van so you can litter it with your OWN child's French fries and melted crayons.
- If I don't have a snack in the car at school pickup, it's not pretty.
- You can't pull gum out of hair; you have to CUT it out.
- I have another child named "Not Me" living in my house.
- There IS a difference between boys and girls.
- My daughters can pull each other's hair harder than I could pull my sister's hair.
- It is easier to read *War and Peace* than to get a child to apologize to their sibling.
- You can't turn the sound of your car stereo up high enough to drown out kids yelling at each other.
- Girls' clothing does not necessarily cost less than couture apparel.
- I am not in control...

I've replaced my business skills with patience. I've met even more interesting people—kids and their parents. And, most importantly, I know I've contributed to the world by bringing my children into it. I would not give up those four a.m. cuddle moments; that tearstained face with a glimpse of a smile when I'm wiping a scrape where skin met pavement; or that look of accomplishment when my daughters finish putting on a "show." God blessed me with these gifts, and I need to thank him daily. Oh no. I'm sorry to have to run. It's time to thwart World War III in my living room, which, I'm sure, "Not Me" instigated...

∼ A Few Good Men *by Donna B. Jones* ∼

"Yes. You're pregnant," confirmed the nurse. Her lips moved, but all I could hear was my internal voice speaking like actress Butterfly McQueen as the character Prissy, housemaid to Vivien Leigh's Scarlet O'Hara, in "Gone with the Wind." "Oh, Miss Scarlet, I don't know nuthin' 'bout birthin' babies."

In my case, I was 39 years old, a 20-year veteran of news reporting and corporate communications, married nine years with a refurbished home and two dogs in a "Leave It to Beaver"-style neighborhood. I knew all about the business world, microwave popcorn, drive-thrus, the Bravo channel, but nothing about motherhood.

Sure, having a child was a part of the divine plan, but after a few years of trying, I had settled into the notion that I was just going to be one of those nice aunts that everyone talks about at the family reunions. You know, the "why didn't she ever have children" aunts. So the news that I was "with child" was the shock heard round the world (by the reaction of my relatives). Even I was surprised. With two busy professionals living under one roof, sex became those brief brushes against each other in the closet each morning as we grabbed clothes and ran out the door.

Me pregnant? I found myself opening old books and surfing the net for a refresher course on the reproductive system. For the first time, this Type A corporate kid didn't know what to expect. It wouldn't be long before the shock wore off and the Type A personality kicked into gear. There was work to be done! Little did I know that I would soon turn to a few good men for help!

Becoming a mother was all or nothing for me. Give up caffeine—check. Organize nursery—check. Find a new home for my hyperactive dogs—sadly, check (happily it is an open adoption). Attend said baby showers—check. Regular medical checkups—check. Quit work cold turkey to be full-time mother—check. (Remember, it was all or nothing, and my husband, Brian, willingly took the traditional lead role in the breadwinning department. Enter "good man" number one!)

Finally my newest little "client" arrived. When my son's eyes looked into mine, it was magic. This was the one moment that truly lived up to its public relations hype. It was as perfect and emotional as they come, but times they were a changing. In just a matter of hours, this former corporate executive had given up control of her heart and home to a 10-pound butterball. I was now the "intern," learning on the job without pay, without fringe benefits, and taking orders from a little fellow who was equally green to the ways of this world.

It wasn't long before I realized that I should have paid closer attention to those child-rearing bibles people give you at baby showers, instead of letting nature take its course. I knew I was in trouble when my solo performance with the breast pump turned sour. For the first time in my life, I finally learned what those appendages were for, and they were not just to look good in a two-piece Chanel number! From the way the hospital nurses talked, I thought breast-feeding my child would leave me cast with a golden hue, tiny birds chirping in harmony and orchestra music in the background. I had no idea it was more like Old MacDonald and his farm as I sat strapped to a breast pump like poor ol' Bessy!

I needed a pep talk on parenthood, like a rookie needs pointers from a coach. Call my parents or in-laws? What, and admit that at my age, I hadn't a clue? Talk with my sister? Yes, that helped, but you had to be prepared for the follow-up pop quiz. Ask friends? In the beginning, it's a pride thing. So, when my husband returned to work, I bravely waved good-bye at the door, our little bundle of joy in hand. I smiled as his car pulled away, secretly whispering, "Don't go!" I was tired, smelly, and losing my footing already. I needed a safety net, a booster shot, and a shot of tequila—something!

Suddenly, there he was...the pool man. No, it's not what you think. This guy is a married father of three, and that means he knows stuff about kids! So there I was, running outside to greet my new best friend, Dave, armed not with thoughts on how to improve the color and clarity of our pool water but with questions about kids.

"When did your kids finally sleep through the night? When did yours learn how to crawl? What formula did you use?" were just a few of my weighted greetings. I could care less if the pool had algae growing in it. I needed answers, man!

Dave was quick to oblige, as if I had asked him to share with me his list of top ten sports teams. He'd give me the stats on how he and his wife coped with lifestyle changes when their children were born, tips on how to know when your child is ready to crawl, and so on.

Next came the county water inspector. Once I found out he was a dad, he was fair game. He was a farm-raised southern man in his late 50s who spoke about body parts like he does water pipes—their function to get the job done. "My wife breast-fed the kids until they were toddlers," he boasted, "but it's not for everyone. Your kid will grow up big and strong, you watch!" Yes, that's right. I went from helping clients with corporate imaging to talking with a stranger, a male stranger, about the pros and cons of breast-feeding children. The funny thing about all of this was that these guys didn't hesitate to talk about being dads, about life with their kids, and about their selfless wives! Who knew?

Bob, the mailman, would add his two cents as I ran out to the mailbox in search of diaper coupons or my next issue of *Parents* magazine. Richard, our lawn expert, would give a plug for the armed forces as he boasted about his son's accomplishments. Delivery guys wouldn't ring the doorbell during standard naptimes (without a word from me). It's like they had a sixth sense! From diapers and diets to playtime techniques and potty-training tips, these unlikely resources became my new "dream team!" With my pep talks complete and my confidence restored, I took on motherhood like I would handle a tough client—believing in myself.

When that breast pump ran dry, I popped open a can of ready-made formula and told myself to move on. One by one, I began to take them all on—nasty diapers ("Just hold your breath, and there's nothing to it," said Jake, the pest control man), spit-up ("Depending on what you feed him, the color can often blend in nicely with what you're wearing," joked Mike, the plumber), finding time to take showers..."Well, that's why God invented deodorant, right?" chuckled my dad. Sleepless nights were a whole other beast, which is what I looked like after being up for 48 hours straight. My husband was my knight in shining armor in that arena, taking on those crazy late-night baby-feeding shifts even with a full workday ahead.

There were supermen all around me—even at the grocery store. For stay-at-home mothers, a trip to the grocery store is like a trip to Disney World! Granted, there are women walking around like they stepped out of the movie "Stepford Wives," eyes fixed and smiles firmly painted on their faces as children screamed, reached, pulled, tugged, whined, and climbed on everything that wasn't nailed down. Let's get real. Smiling isn't the cure for the baby blues. We all need help...Supermarket clerks to the rescue—mostly retired gentlemen working to make ends meet. To "us moms" they might as well be wearing red capes with a big letter "S" on their chests. They are quick to act, whipping out a balloon from behind their backs or catching a frustrated child off guard by looking them in the eyes and asking, "Are you having a bad day?" Then they whisk us off to our cars, help us pack up our purchases while we strap in our children, and before we can turn around to say thank you, they're gone.

Sure, there are dozens of other natural heroes in this story—baby-sitting grandparents, siblings with endless advice, friends, and so on—but it's the kindness of some unlikely rescuers that turned this ex-exec and desperate housewife into a daring new mom. I no longer fear spit-up but wear it as a badge of honor. After all, as Jim the septic man says, "When a two-ton elephant sits in the middle of your living room, you just have to laugh." Enough said.

∾ Sick and Tired *by Queta Gavin* ∾

If I had a dime for every time I've heard, "Be careful what you wish for," I wouldn't be a millionaire, but I would be able to purchase a nice pair of Manolo Blahniks. Yes, I'd heard it, but I didn't heed it. The summer of 1998, on my 42nd birthday, I fervently wished to leave the ranks of the gainfully employed. I was sick and tired of my job.

Don't get me wrong. I'm not a lazy chick. Since age 14, I have always held some kind of job, sometimes two. Early on, I developed a strong work ethic. I had to. Dear old Dad was not very forthcoming with the funds when it came to his five daughters. By age 12, I had already realized my passion for and obsession with shoes. This, of course, fueled my need for my own cash. Having a job gave me this heady feeling of importance and independence.

In my quest for the almighty dollar and more shoes, I've worked as a cashier, secretary, typesetter, data entry operator, food service person, salesperson, customer service rep, model, dancer, and even worked part-time in a shoe store. Imagine that. While a single mother of two daughters, Yolanda and Quiana, I returned to college and attained better positions with higher wages. I soon began my most and least favorite job: administrative director of a manufacturing company. This was the position that ultimately made me wish for a life without a timesheet.

I stumbled into the job. I was working as an assistant to the president of a manufacturing company in Detroit when he decided to start a new company in Georgia. Jack offered me a sizeable salary and moving expenses as an enticement to relocate and help him start this new company. He happened to catch me at the right time. I had always wanted to move back south and live in the Atlanta area. Quiana's daddy lived there, and it was also a way to escape the long, cold, gloomy winters of Detroit. So, one week before the Christmas of 1993, I packed up my then eight-year-old daughter Quiana, my 50 pair of shoes, and headed to Baxley, Georgia in the New South.

Now, you would have thought that this intelligent, well-heeled individual would have done some research on a place that she had never heard of or seen on the news or in the papers. But, noooooooooo. I did the unthinkable. I assumed that it was a suburb of Atlanta. Wrong.

Baxley was so far from Atlanta, it might as well have been in the jungles of South America. Baxley, Georgia, small town USA with a population of maybe 3,000 folks, is located west of Savannah and about 400 miles south of Atlanta. Yahoo! Was I ever dumbfounded. The night I drove into this two-traffic-light town, I almost went into shock. Can you say culture shock? The next morning while grocery shopping at the downtown Winn-Dixie, I noticed that some of my fellow shoppers were walking around the store in their bare feet. As in no shoes. Dorothy, you are no longer in Kansas. It threw me back into culture shock. I realized that my extensive shoe collection would be wasted on this group. To say that we stuck out like sore thumbs would be like saying Bill Gates and Donald Trump are "well-off."

After the initial shock subsided, I threw myself into the task at hand. Jack and I transformed an empty building into a thriving business. The plant was up and running, manufacturing commercial modular units. I felt such a sense of accomplishment. The company had become my life. I worked very long hours, which didn't bother me at first since there wasn't much else to do. Metropolitan Baxley didn't offer very much in the way of entertainment. There were no movie theaters, only Gary's Videos. No restaurants other than the Dairy Queen, Village Pizza, Hardee's, and Mickey D's. In the words of Quiana, "Mama, they don't even have a Wal-Mart or Kmart." So I worked hard during the week and ventured into surrounding cities like Savannah and Jacksonville on the weekends. When Quiana started competing in gymnastics, we were required to travel to Atlanta for her meets. These trips also afforded me a chance to de-stress and journey through DSW, a shoe aficionado's paradise.

Anyone who has worked in human resources can tell you how stressful it can be when you're responsible for employees' wages and benefits. Multiply that by ten at our company. I dreaded Friday paydays.

Folks would lose their mind if even one hour was missing from their check. Usually it would be someone who had selective amnesia about the two days they had "laid out." If, indeed, there was a mistake on my part, it would've been customary to make the adjustment in the next check. Want to bet? They would threaten to kick my lanky behind, quit their job, or go to the Department of Labor. So I always kept some petty cash handy. It was easier and safer that way. Damage my Enzo Angiolinis in a brawl? I think not.

I found that in this small town factory environment, I had unwittingly taken on the role of a social worker. I interacted with the employees on a personal level that normally would not have been required. The employees really worked my nerves. One day, one of the guys entered my office and asked if he could "knock off early." His reason was that his wife had just called and needed him to bring home some sanitary pads. I told him that unless he was bleeding, he'd better head back out to the Flooring Department. I kid you not. I could write a ten-volume encyclopedia on the reasons they were late, couldn't come to work, or just behaved poorly.

I hated, hated, hated this part of my job. Hate is a strong word, and I think that thou shall not hate is a commandment. But I hated that, in order to get a day's work from the employees, I would have to sometimes leave the office to give them a ride to work. If they were in jail, go bail them out. If by Monday they had spent their weekly paycheck, I would add their names to my personal little black book of employee loans. To get an honest day's work from the majority of them, I had to be nurse, counselor, disciplinarian, bail bondsman, chauffeur, minister, and loan officer. What I hated most was through all of this, they despised and resented me. But we do what we must. I must admit there were times I'd get so disgusted, I'd feel an overwhelming urge to take off one of my pumps and just start whaling away and beating some good old-fashioned common sense into everybody. I wouldn't have used one of my Via Spigas, though.

Eventually and inevitably, Jack and I turned our professional relationship into a personal one, became engaged, and moved in together. We were already outsiders. So double the stress of dating the boss, and then triple that with being an interracial couple in a town of small-minded Southern Baptists and rednecks. Never mind that the plant had provided over 175 well-paying jobs to the people in the area. We would always be outsiders. If not for the hospitality and friendship of Jackie, a native of Baxley, and for my daily 1-800 calls to my sister friends, Tracie in Detroit and Sheila in Rochester, I think that the ostracism and isolation surely would have taken their toll on me.

Skip to five years later, and I was chomping at the bit to move to darn near anywhere. Well, maybe not Iowa. Since we couldn't find anyone competent to run the business, we were held captive in Baxley. In an attempt to provide Quiana with a quality education and broaden her horizons, we enrolled her in the Bolles School in Jacksonville as a five-day boarder. I would make the four-and-a-half hour round-trip drive to pick her up Friday and take her back on Sunday. I missed her so much during the week, though I was still putting in very long hours at the office. I had recently purchased a house that was being renovated. That in itself was a challenging endeavor given the locals' poor work ethic. Not surprisingly, the neighbors didn't bring us cakes to welcome us to the neighborhood. I hated the turn my life had taken.

For my 40th birthday, Jack bought me a two-week timeshare in Hilton Head, South Carolina so that my friends from Detroit could come down to celebrate with me. He knew how terribly I missed them. So, annually for two weeks, my friends would meet me there. We enjoyed bicycling, shopping, partying, and hanging out at the beach and poolside. The summer of my 42nd birthday, I was so exhausted that I didn't want to do anything but sleep. I clearly remember blowing out my candles and wishing that I didn't have to work anymore. I was so exhausted. I was sick of working. I was sick of everything. I soon learned that I was just sick.

I hadn't missed a day of work in five years. Soon I was missing work, days at a time with flu-like symptoms. A new infection invaded my body weekly. Antibiotics were useless, and by the time I was alerted to get admitted to the hospital immediately, I was in a life-threatening situation. I could barely hold my head up, let alone walk. After more blood work and a bone marrow biopsy, I was finally able to attribute my debilitating fatigue, bruises, and infections to acute myelogenous leukemia.

The doctor delivered this news to me rather callously by rattling off statistics and a bleak prognosis. I didn't care what he said. I didn't even cry. All I wanted to know was what I needed to do to get well. Yolanda, my eldest, was already out on her own, so I didn't worry about her as much. But Quiana was only 13, and I didn't want anyone else to have to raise her. That was my first and most important job. As I said, I didn't cry. Not for one moment did I entertain the thought that I might die. Hell, I had over 80 pair of size nines at home I had yet to wear.

After being hospitalized for months to receive aggressive chemotherapy, I went into remission. A year and six months later, it was back. My only hope for survival was a bone marrow transplant. I didn't have a donor, so after more chemotherapy, total body radiation, infected catheters, and all the other horrific crap that comes with cancer, I had a stem cell transplant. With the Almighty Healer, a super supportive group of caregivers, and an unwavering faith, I kicked AML's butt again. I am a miracle. Three years post transplant, and I have not had so much as a cold. I have the bones and stamina of a much older person due to so much chemo and radiation. But I'm here.

I guess you can say my wish had come true. I never returned to my job. In fact, I haven't held a full-time job since December 1, 1998. My bouts of debilitating fatigue make it almost impossible for me to hold a job. My income now consists of a paltry, monthly Social Security disability check. Jack and I are no longer together, Quiana is in her sophomore year at Florida Southern College, Yolanda lives in Rochester, and I have moved in with my Aunt Carolyn back home in Detroit. I've come full circle, and I am so much happier.

I must admit the transition from working to staying at home was a difficult pill to swallow. I thrive on activity and sometimes border on hyper. Though I love reading, watching TV, and doing crosswords, they just weren't doing it for me. Even frequent shoe-shopping sprees didn't help. I was bored to tears. I wore out the 800 lines to my sister friends' jobs. I called so much that they had to remind me that, unlike me, they had to work. I had gotten my wish, and I still wasn't satisfied, mainly because I had defined myself through my job. Before, if someone asked me what I did, I could proudly tell him or her. Now that I didn't have a job, I felt worthless and useless. I felt that I had lost Queta. One day, I called Jack at work, bawling because "I didn't feel like me anymore."

Never one to stay at a pity party very long, I got active. With my limited stamina, I went out and started a new career. So now if someone asks me what I do, I simply state, I am a volunteer. I love volunteering.

I find it extremely fulfilling and a great way to express my creative side. Through the Leukemia and Lymphoma Society, I have finished a 26.2-mile marathon, raising almost $5,000. I speak at events, and I have appeared on television, radio, and a billboard promoting the Society. As a "first connector," I share my experience with new leukemia patients and volunteer two days a week in the office.

While in Jacksonville, I was an active member of the Wolfsons Children's Hospital auxiliary. As a "pink lady," I worked with the teen patients because the older ladies preferred working with the smaller children. I had a blast, and they enjoyed the activities I planned for them. I attended beauty school and received my license as a nail technician and incorporated this into my visits with the girls in the hospital. They loved getting their nails polished. I kept the dialysis patients so busy that their three to four hours on the machines passed more rapidly. They would give me the third degree if I missed a Wednesday.

I got Quiana on the bandwagon, and through her own organization, Kindred Spirits, we delivered money, tabs, and supplies to the local Ronald McDonald House and other causes. It was through my volunteerism that I was honored in Washington DC as one of the "Eckerd 100," women across the country recognized for their volunteer efforts.

Be careful what you wish for, indeed. Even though my wish was granted, by way of a life-altering disease, I think it is one of the best things that could have happened to me. I know some people might not get it when I say this. Yes, kicking cancer twice was no walk in the park. And yes, my lifestyle drastically changed. I lost two homes, two cars, and a lot of purchasing power. But I've gained so much more. While I was ill, all I wanted was to feel well again. At one point, I truly believed that I would never feel really good again. Then, one day, I woke up and I said to myself, "Self, damn I feel good!" After that, everything else has been gravy.

I have a better sense of who I am and that my purpose in life is to help others. I'm learning to be more patient and less judgmental. I no longer confuse my wants with my needs. I don't need a paycheck to feel good about myself. Most importantly, I understand what is important in life—people, not things. I try so hard to impart this bit of knowledge to others. I'm blessed to have free time to spend with my girls, friends, and relatives.

Recently, I had the honor of being caregiver to a favorite cousin in Fort Lauderdale. Sadly, Jackie fought a hard and painful but losing battle with pancreatic cancer. Watching her die has been one of the hardest things I've ever had to do. But I feel blessed for it. I know I am a miracle. I thank God daily and try to live my life with that thought in mind. I've beat cancer, but doggone it to hell, I still can't beat my shoe obsession. Did somebody say shoe sale?

∾ **What's in a Name?** *by Jennifer Hamman* ∾

We have all heard the expression, "What's in a name?" Well, for me, that saying has been changed many times. In the beginning, I was Jennifer Garwood, graduate of Western Kentucky University, out to save the world as a first-class therapist. This was accomplished when I received the directorship of head of alternative therapies at my first hospital. Yes, that is a feel-good title. There were two of us, and the other person was part-time, but still, I was in charge.

Then came the next name: Mrs. James Hamman. Let me tell you, I am as proud as ever to wear it and continue to wear it, not an easy feat in these times of divorce. I still, however, was continuing to add to my corporate titles. There came director of psych utilization review and then a move.

My husband's company offered him a move that would be great for his career, but for me, it was a little more difficult to find positions. So what's a girl to do? "Ah," career change. If you have ever worked in the mental health field, then you will know a little change can be good for your mental health. So here came name number four. My husband and I had been remodeling houses and selling them, two so far and working on number three. So, what better career choice than real estate agent? This worked well. I listed a few, sold a few, and then here came another move. But this time, I get one big sale before I leave town. My own house sold in three days...my claim to fame as an agent.

Now, time for name number five. What do you do when you move to a state where all your past lives don't seem to fit? "Recreate" again. We are now working on house number four, I have no job, and my husband is being worked to the bone. But, I can't worry about that. I need a mop. So, I go to this very unique houseware shop to find a mop, and instead what I find is a job. Now, let me introduce myself: assistant manager to a great store doing extremely fun things like display designs and going into New York on buying sprees for the store.

And then comes the BIGGEST change of my life. I'm going to be a MOM. My husband and I had always said when we have kids we wanted me to be able to stay at home. So, after many name changes, the one that I currently have is stay-at-home mom. Who knew this one would be the hardest job to date? Yes, I get to be the boss, but the employees seem to always get the last word. There are no employee handbooks or human resource seminars. My husband is still being worked to the bone and is the "Good Guy" in the eyes of the little employees. Too bad you can't write them up! Yes, there is time out, but who is that really punishing?

For a woman who was always organized, on time, balls-to-the-wall on the go, the switch was like whiplash. Not feeling organized in my brain or in my house...one empty diaper bag, lost shoe, or refusal to wear clothes put me in a tailspin. And forget being on time. Fifteen minutes late, and I consider us still in the ballpark. For the few cavemen who think we sit around eating the perpetual bonbon, ten minutes with my crew will have them crying like the true wimps they are on an easy day. But no matter how I might complain at times (and, according to my husband, that can be often, on a bad day), I would not give up my choice to stay home. With one "I LOVE YOU," my little angel reminds me of why, with all the names I had, MOM is one that will never change. The few years that I have her all to myself are priceless. My "salary" is watching her learn something new, grow a little taller, and repeat that word you wish you hadn't said. Nothing will ever replace that feeling. Lastly, to my husband, who is still working himself to the bone, THANK YOU.

∾ From Boardroom to Baby *by Ieshia Ali* ∾

Thinking back, it was then that I decided to change the trajectory of my career. Seated in the plush leather high back chair around the cherry wood conference table adorned with dazzling flowers and fresh food, I took in the vibrant sails gliding past the Opera House. The landmark Sydney Opera House, smaller than I first imagined, was, however, a lovely distraction from the self-important banter flying around my head. In the penthouse boardroom of this skyscraper, I was smart enough to tag a chair opposing the floor-to-ceiling windows. This was a five-day meeting, including all relevant managers governing the operations of the Asia Pacific region of this French conglomerate, and it dragged on and on. I was the youngest, the only female, solo American, and no longer enamored with this "fantastic" career of a lifetime.

This was the third day of a six-week residency on my fifth expedition to the region in 2.5 years, and I had already handed in my mental resignation. Engineering and Operations was not my joie de vive, and at the tender age of 27, I was adamant that something had to give. As the regional sales director, a petite Frenchman—much less arrogant than my group manager and a lot more personable—stood near the projection wall, pointing at optimistic and completely unfounded quarterly extrapolations, my mind escaped the confines of this place yet again. The Harbor Bridge situated to the left of this picture window looked like a massive jungle gym with tourists climbing up and down its assembled steel, connected only by a rope and common daredevil desires. With fondness in my glazed eyes, I remembered my time on the bridge, back when I was captivated by this city, my job, and life's possibilities. Funny thing is, it was only two years ago. Too many corporate disillusions in such a contracted span of time will do that to someone. You know, shove them out of love or even like of their career, or just maybe over the bridge into the harbor.

As usual, I racked up the sky miles from Sydney to Auckland to Tokyo then Singapore, with a respite in Langkawi, Malaysia. Then there was more business in Singapore and Hong Kong before returning to the ocean city of Sydney. I really missed my boyfriend. The pleasure of his smile was on hiatus. I was across the world, experiencing exotic and sometimes frightening things, all alone. My stereotypical French boss and his Laotian "yes-man" were not my idea of traveling companions. They weren't even my idea of coworkers.

The one thing that helped keep my spirits up was shopping! The dollar was strong, and I had lots of them. The yen dug deep into my pockets, but Hong Kong and Sydney helped improve my mood. I begged my main man to take a contract. He was an independent consultant in Sydney. We could have lived like royalty. He balked, and I returned to my homeland and my lover.

To my surprise, as one door was slowly closing, another was creeping open. My main man was just as ready for a change of life as I had become, or at least he thought so. We bought and renovated an old Washington, DC row house, became engaged, and got married—all in the following year. Whew! What a whirlwind of 12 months. I would not suggest such vigorous activity to anyone. Let's just say there were therapists and prescriptions involved. I abandoned the notion of pharmaceutical aid and found my way back to yoga. At the time, I didn't realize what a blessing and significant part of my life this discipline would become.

Throughout our courtship, my husband and I sustained a commuter relationship. My girlfriends couldn't believe that I considered myself whole and fulfilled without having my mate at arm's reach seven days a week. I always found it odd that they would consistently demand the attention and presence of their partners. To each their own. But, of course, the news that free spirit me would actually jump the broom and take a groom dazed and intrigued them all. Secretly, I relished any opportunity to add shock value. I don't consider myself a rebel, but one of my favorite quotes would be by Malcolm X: "The road to freedom is seldom traveled by the masses." So yes, this wild child was settling down, with a Muslim man to boot...more shock value!

Within six months of the wedding, the glow of "newlywedism" had faded to black. Life as a single person during the week versus partying lovebird on the weekend was taking its toll on this 29-year-old corporate burnout. Hubby and I talked about finally consolidating households. We would convert our newly renovated city pad into a rental property, and I would finally make the move to Philadelphia where he had been on a long-term contract. There was some resistance by my partner to actually begin our marriage—you know, living together, sharing finances, starting a family. It seemed he really hadn't thought through the logistics of merging our separate lives into a single joint venture. Well, I had, and ready-or-not, off we went. I had recently joined him as a 30-something, picked up my life, and moved to a foreign city— not so scary for me, but leaving my friends and financial independence, well, that was a bitter pill to swallow.

Little did I know then that life was about to become a bit more daunting.

Shortly after the transplant shock subsided, I found that my ovulation tracking software, fertility OPK kits, and Nazi-like cervical mucous checks finally yielded the desired result. Just six months post birth control pill abandonment, and we were pregnant! Like many first-time preggers, I went overboard with the announcement to hubby. There were pink and blue balloons, my Elmo doll—yes, Elmo—holding the positive pg test stick in the pocket of his overalls. (Elmo wore 0/3-month overalls.).

I was even more ecstatic to find that the dreaded morning sickness seemed to elude me with every week that went by. Nothing more than super exhaustion and occasionally a sharp, debilitating pain on my left side. It only happened twice during my sixth and eighth weeks, and it would retreat as swiftly as it appeared. Not even the agony of those sharp pains dismayed my elation that my life was on an altered course, a married soon-to-be-mommy. Almost no one could believe this was me.

Shortly upon relocating to Pennsylvania, I began the dreaded job search. I wasn't so much looking to re-enter the corporate arena, but this SAHW (stay-at-home wife) thing wasn't as shiny and bright as it seemed from the other side of the playing field. My husband had a life in Pennsylvania, and I didn't and desperately needed one. However, after the pregnancy news, the search traversed to locating an OB-GYN.

Can I tell you what an eye-opening experience this was? Man, healthcare in America is in deep trouble if you ask me. It took four referrals from wives of men I barely knew and four weeks to finally confirm an OB appointment. Week ten and two days would be my first eagerly anticipated appointment. Week ten and zero days, I began bleeding bright red blood. I had ignored my intuitive suspicion regarding the previous two weeks of dark brown spotting. Various sources—cyber chat clubs and mommy-to-be books—had assured me that old brown blood was less suspicious than fresh red blood. Boy, was I right that something was wrong.

Two emergency rooms later, four doctors, a surgeon, one less fallopian tube, two pints of blood, one week in the hospital, and four weeks of no driving or exercise as I lay all alone on the coach, popping OxyContin and waiting for my stitches to dissolve—my mind drifted back to my final days in Asia. "Life wasn't so bad, little girl," I thought to myself. "Sure, the men I worked with were jerks, but I knew how to handle them. Maybe you weren't designed for this particular calling," my mind continued on this path. "You may not have liked your career, but at least you were good at it." Okay, so I stopped taking the OxyContin and stuck to the 800mg Ibuprofen—much less taxing on the brain and emotions.

But I must say, the healing process was a mountain to climb. I really wanted to be pregnant, have a baby, and be a mother. I always got what I wanted, but this time I was humbled instead of rewarded.

One year and one month later, I found myself being rewarded in a way I never anticipated. I, the yoga preaching/teaching, natural childbirth advocate, was being put through her paces at The Birth Center. Thirty-one hours of active labor elapsed before everyone was tired, and we schlepped across the street to the hospital for Pitocin and drug relief. Seven hours after that, my reward was in hand. He was pushed out in 30 minutes, all seven pounds, seven ounces, bright-eyed and a carbon copy of my own newborn picture!

"Oh my God," after noting the immediate physical relief that washed over me, "this is how it happens. I'm a part of the circle of life." Smiling inside, I was proud to have conquered this rite of passage. Those doubts about my fertility and worthiness to become a mom softened with each waning contraction.

So, not only am I a SAHW, I've added SAHM to my list of credentials. The journey has been awesome. In just 13 months, I have reacquainted myself with many positive characteristics of the old me that I mistakenly thought had no place in my "new" life, as well as discovered elements of my new evolving self. I must admit, it took some time for me to actually feel like I was NOT baby-sitting, that indeed, this is my son. It took me a while to realize that sleeping in no longer exists; forget about it for now and don't be resentful.

On the other hand, I smile like Ronald McDonald when watching my little man try to run from his father who's chasing him on all fours, or when he "looks" for me behind my hands as we play peek-a-boo. I also preen with pride as I reply, "yes" when asked if I still breast-feed or when my yoga students congregate around my little man after class even though he squealed all the way through savasana.

There has now been enough distance, kind of like labor, that I can look at my career and highlight the idyllic memories, foregoing the less favorable aspects like the mind-numbing meetings on situations that will never change. My new career offers me the position of teacher and student on a daily basis. Together we unfold our mutual biographies, one day at a time. And, oh yeah, I had almost forgotten how intriguing an old set of house keys can be!

∼ Do Moms Work? *by Brenda Jurbala* ∼

I am a physical therapist and worked in the therapy field until I had my first child, now 11. Shortly after he was born, I did return to work five days per week for about four hours each day for only about four months. I was helping out a previous employer for a short time. I continued to stay at home after that until my son was about two and a half years old. At that time, I went back to work for two years because we were fearful that my husband might lose his job. After that, I again returned home to work as a full-time mom.

Since then, we have adopted two beautiful girls from China, and I continue to be a full-time mom. My oldest daughter, now four, had great dreams for herself about entering the workforce as an adult but was somewhat confused about the role of women! Shortly after she turned three, she decided that she was going to be a ballerina and a doctor. Of course, we encouraged her and told her she could do anything! As time passed, she announced that she was going to be a ballerina and doctor and that her workplace would be in the office where Daddy worked. Again, we praised her for her dreams! Time continued to pass, and her thoughts apparently continued to dwell on her dreams of a great career. She then announced that when she became a ballerina and a doctor, not only would she work at Daddy's office, but she would also be a man! I curiously asked her why she would be a man, and she told me that she had to be a man if she wanted to work. After all, Mommy does not leave the house to work, so apparently in her mind that meant that no women leave the home to work!

My daughter's point of view may be a little twisted, and this may even make some women think that I am not setting a good example of what a woman can be, but I do not. It is difficult being a stay-at-home mom. Not only because I almost never get to see other adults, but also because sometimes my self-esteem dwindles because I am not out there pursuing a career and "bettering" myself. I tend to look down on myself at times or think that others will look down on me because I am "just staying at home."

But I overcame those thoughts, and I know that what I am doing is the best I can for my family. I know that when my children are grown, they will appreciate what I am doing for them. My husband makes a good income, but it is sometimes tempting to think of what it could be if I went back to work! Yet, there is no question in our minds that the best choice we have for our family is for me to work in the home and care for our kids. I only have six and a half years left before my son goes to college, and I know how quickly that time will fly! Even when our girls start school, I will probably only go back to work part-time, since I want to be involved in their school just as I was for my son. I think when my kids grow up, they are going to be able to say, "I had a great childhood," and that is what I will feel the most proud of.

∼ A Workaholic Gone Good *by Camie Dunbar* ∼

When I was a little girl, my mother was a stay-at-home mom. She was always there for my sister, brother, and me...volunteering at our school, taking us to after-school activities, helping us with our homework, and the list goes on. Although I appreciated having her there, I always said I could never be like her. I wanted more out of my life, and I set out as a small girl ready to climb that corporate ladder.

Although my goal was to be the first woman astronaut or the first female president (yes, that's how I dressed on career day, and I have pictures to prove it), my first job was actually as a waitress in an ice cream parlor at the age of 15. I always saved my money and continued to come up with creative ways to make even more. I felt the more money I had, the more successful I would be.

I went on to college and set out to conquer the world. I had no desire to get married and definitely no desire to have children. I wanted to be the most successful female executive there ever was; and as my career grew, I was heading in that direction. I started as an assistant promotion director for an upscale women's boutique, then headed to a major fragrance retailer at the age of 22 to assist in their marketing department. By the time I was 25, I was the marketing director for the company, and I was overseeing all marketing aspects for over 320 stores nationwide. (Note: I met my husband while at this company and got married to the man of my dreams—"Oh no, I broke my first rule!")

Of course, I wanted more, so I set out to climb that next rung on the ladder. I found myself running the marketing for four major radio stations in the South Florida market. I was working hard (about 60-80 hours and sometimes more a week) to reach my goal of being the most successful female executive there ever was. My husband always said I lived to work and he worked to live. It was always a sore spot, but he was right!

March 6, 2001 was the day I realized I was heading in the wrong direction. I was in Jackson Hole, Wyoming, overseeing a ski trip for one of my radio stations, and it hit me...or should I say I hit it! It was our last day and our last run, and I was trying to find my way to the bottom of the mountain to prepare for the awards ceremony. On the direction of a Jackson Hole employee, I headed down a catwalk to what I thought was another run. On the contrary, it was a half-pipe with about a 20-foot bottom. My life flashed before me as I headed over the lip of the half-pipe and came crashing down on the hard-packed ice with my left leg hitting first. My pelvis was shattered, and, almost, so was my life.

I was airlifted to Denver Medical Center, where I spent about three weeks being operated on (my pelvis is now made up of 22 screws, three plates, and a total hip replacement), receiving numerous blood transfusions, and being rehabilitated. My family was told that I was lucky to be alive.

As I spent months in a wheelchair, at doctors' offices and physical therapy, I had a lot of time to think about my future. Some told me I had to be prepared that I might never walk again, or I might never be able to have children or live the active lifestyle I once enjoyed. All of those thoughts hit home with me. Have I really accomplished what I set out to be? The answer was NO!

The true answer is that I really set out to be just like my mother, but I never really knew it. I am happy to say that I am walking, and I am the proud mother of two-year-old Madison, and we have one on the way (yes, I broke rule #2). Because I was forced to take better care of myself, I decided after three months back in the rat race of Corporate America, my goal in life was to work from home so I could be the best mother I could be, just like my mother was to us. Do you know what I have found? It's the most demanding but the most rewarding job I have ever held. I thank my mom for showing me the way to true happiness!

CHAPTER 5

IT TAKES A VILLAGE, BUT SOMETIMES I WANT TO LEAVE MINE

~ **Meet and Greet** by Melissa Rajsky ~

Making the leap from businesswoman to suburban mom has stripped a seasoned corporate veteran down to the core of myself so I can rebuild from the ground up as a stay-at-home mommy. My credentials mean nil. My former business conquests and accomplishments are useless. Even creative talents, humanitarian acts, and death-defying feats will not help me in this new, uncharted territory. I am a "newbie" in my suburban mommy terrain. Unacceptable to the other inhabitants until I earn my wings through amazing gourmet treats created for snack day, superior organization skills for carpool-schedule juggling, and a half a million hours of selfless, donated time to bake sale event planning and craft production.

This has got me thinking that superiority and condescension are a contest in my suburban neighborhood. Participants of Olympic proportions competing to prove they were exceptional in all things "Mother." Whilst they rest comfortably on their lofty pinnacle, only to cast a disapproving glare at those of us who are getting our first foothold on the steep and treacherous terrain of suburban socialization, they pause only to occasionally throw us a flimsy line. Mostly, they kick a boulder in our way. I have since resigned myself to the conclusion that maybe there is something to make these women more superior to me as a wife and a mother. What if they are governing sovereignty of a small country and are actually prohibited from cavorting with the common people by royal mandate? Possibly, they are heiresses to large family fortunes and are merely biding their time in middle-class suburbia until somebody dies. My favorite reasoning is that they have a special hidden talent, like they can suck a golf ball through a garden hose. This is the answer I find most acceptable, and it certainly would explain why they cannot tilt their heads to acknowledge my presence. All this kidding and complaining aside, you do what you have to do for your kids. Somehow, some way, you have to figure out how to navigate your new life as a mommy. All you have to do is make a good first impression. Or, so you think.

The suburban equivalent to being fresh meat in a corrections facility is the kindergarten meet-and-greet. This is the big dance, the premier event. It is held every year under the pretense of letting your innocent, angel-faced preschooler be surrounded by 75 to 100 children they do not know, in hopes they will immediately bond with them, thus making their first few days of kindergarten less traumatic. What it actually ends up being is a reminder from the upper hierarchy to the rest of us where everyone's place is status wise, ergo where their children's place will be for the upcoming 13 years of school.

Undaunted by this upcoming event, partly because I am still riding high on the wave of my corporate standings and partly because living as a suburban mom has started to impair my ability to reason like a normal human being, I devise a method to break down this wall standing in the way of my child's happiness. I am, after all, a businesswoman. So, I figure treating motherhood like any other business would be the secret to success. I ask myself, "How would I approach a new client or colleague?" I would offer a firm handshake, look them straight in the eye, speak clearly, not ramble on, and quickly establish common ground. Piece of cake. These "Mothers" are sure to warm up to my no-nonsense, confident approach.

We know a few children when we arrive, so we establish a safe base camp from which to operate. Usually these meets are held at someone's estate; this one is at the local country club. A visual reminder from the upper hierarchy of where your place is and that it is not here. Eager to test my theory, I convince my unsuspecting, nearly five-year-old to take a lap around the party. We spot two moms with children who will be in my son's class. We can tell by the efficient color-coded name tags everyone is wearing. They look friendly and approachable. As we near the two women, I recognize one of them from when I worked out at the YMCA, *and* she's friends with someone I know in my neighborhood—jackpot.

"Hello," I say and proceed to introduce my son and myself. After we let our children blink and stare at each other for a few moments, I turn to Mom-I-recognize and say, "Didn't you use to work out at the Y?"

At first she seemed startled that I would address her directly; then she gave her chum a sidelong look and flatly replied, "I still do." The other mother now has a big, uncomfortable smile frozen on her face like she is about to witness a social train wreck. Do I detect the slightest movement of her head? It's almost like she is shaking her head to warn me. I go ahead anyway and throw out my second attempt to make contact.

"Aren't you friends with so-and-so?"

This one causes her to actually take a step back and produce an annoyed, "Yes, very good friends." Her icy tone, lack of elaboration, and the fact that she has turned away from me signifies that this meet-and-greet has come to a conclusion.

I look down at my son, smarting from my failure, and see how uncomfortable I have made him. Luckily, he has spotted some ice cream in the clubhouse; dousing our sorrows in a double scoop is just the ticket. We pick out our favorites, and the Ralph Lauren poster boy behind the counter pulls out an official-looking pad and asks if we are members.

"Not even close," I sheepishly admit. He looks at our already licked ice cream and then checks around the clubhouse. When he confirms the coast is clear, he nods toward the door and lets us go, free of charge. My son and I wander away from the rest of the party, down by the lake to discover an amazing view with front row seats in large Adirondack chairs. As we look through towering palm trees to bright blue sky, we see how many things we can spot in the puffy clouds.

"I see bunny rabbit," he says.

"I see Scooby Doo," I say.

"Do not!" He immediately realizes my fib. I catch a glimpse of my son's beautiful, happy face and suddenly realize I've already made it to the top of the heap. It's not about who I impress, it's what I imprint on my son's recollection of his childhood that counts, and I almost missed it completely.

∼ Love Thy Neighbor? ∼
by Lisa Manrique Spengler

Actually, it's "love thy neighbor as yourself." God certainly couldn't have meant for me to love my neighbors, could He? This surely can be a hard commandment to teach our children, especially if we live close to someone who just seems so unlovable. But, like many parents, we try our best to do the right thing and lead by example no matter how sticky things get. I wonder if loving your neighbors just when they deserve it is enough?

At first, when we moved into our new home last year, everyone seemed so nice. In the cul-de-sac of Mackenzie Way, we often ordered gourmet pizza or grilled out with our new neighbors. To get the weekend happy hour off to a start, the guys whipped up margaritas for the moms, while they downed their bottled beer. The grown-ups coordinated who would bring what for our potluck dinners and decided which guy would be in charge of grilling. All of the 11 kids between us enjoyed having free reign of the cul-de-sac, backyard play sets, and our ever-popular trampoline. Besides the given circumstance of an occasional dispute over not sharing a favorite toy or accidentally hurting someone's feelings, everyone seemed to get along so well. I really felt that we were richly blessed to have such great neighbors. Loving them and their children as I loved myself, and my own kids, was a piece of cake!

My kids were happy to have so many instant playmates at our new home. They raced to the front door when the doorbell rang because they knew it meant they were being included for play time in the front yard, and they didn't want to miss out on any of the action. Everyone gathered to play kickball, ride scooters or bikes, draw sidewalk chalk towns, blow bubbles, or just hang out with each other. While the kids spent carefree days just being kids, the stay-at-home moms swapped our favorite recipes and chatted about the latest school happenings or bunco club gossip. Life in our new little cove seemed so perfect! We really loved our new circle of neighbors.

One day, all of our neighbors planned to have dinner together. We created a menu with a New Orleans theme, and I was assigned to bring Bananas Foster for dessert. Everyone was thrilled about our exciting evening plans. Then, we all scattered to carry on with our busy Saturday family plans. My family left our house for an outing and returned late afternoon to rest up and prepare for our dinner with everyone.

Upon our arrival, we found our neighbors already eating without us. Were they not a part of the same conversation that I participated in when detailed plans were made for dinner? Would they purposely start without us, despite the fact that we returned before the supper hour? It was unbelievably so. Instantly, the feelings I experienced toward them were far from love.

Even my two children were shocked to see the festivities going on in the cul-de-sac. They knew we had rushed back from our daily activities just to join everyone for dinner.

"Mommy, why are they eating without us?" said my four-year-old.

"Honey, I guess they thought we weren't joining them tonight," I said as I gritted my teeth and recalled our firm plans set earlier in the day. "I'm sure they didn't mean to leave us out," I added. But, whom was I trying to fool? Even a preschooler with limited knowledge could figure out that was exactly what had happened. The honeymoon period of neighborly love amongst all of us was apparently over. They were having fun, and we were left out in the cold.

When my family entered our home, there sat the pile of 15 bananas that were supposed to be used to prepare the evening dessert with our neighbors. Hurt, frustrated, and now inside our house, we all argued over what to do next. The kids were very forgiving and just wanted to go outside to play with their friends. My husband and I preferred to hide inside and not confront our rude neighbors. We settled for plan B. We wiped the tears from our eyes as we closed the front windows to drown out the sounds of laughter coming from the cul-de-sac. Then, we watched a movie as a family, ate leftovers for dinner, and prepared lots of Bananas Foster for dessert.

Because of this experience, every day began getting harder for me to treat my neighbors as myself. I knew that my feelings were truly justified, yet I also realized things might get worse before they got better. Soon, the invitations to join them for dinner stopped coming altogether. The doorbell ringing was silenced, too. It wasn't that the gatherings weren't occurring; rather, we were no longer included in them. We sadly watched the casserole dishes being carried from house to house or the kids running through the sprinkler in the front yard and wondered why suddenly we were excluded from the group. How could they be so obvious about ignoring our family? And, how could they justify to their kids that this terrible example of excluding someone is okay?

While I used the unpleasant encounter to teach my kids that two wrongs don't make a right, their kids were soaking in all of their nasty habits like a sponge. My kids and I continued treating them with kindness, even though they would seldom reciprocate. We were as nice as we could possibly be to these people, because I insisted on being a good neighbor and doing the right thing. We invited their kids to jump on our trampoline, play in our backyard, and even join us for dinner. Yet, I still really found it hard to love these neighbors. After all, these were the very people who had been so unkind to my children and me over and over again. I still felt a twinge of fakeness bubbling inside of me whenever I offered a polite invitation. Despite our efforts, they continued to act like meanies.

After I exhausted all of my own ideas on how to remedy this uncomfortable situation, it dawned on me that I needed to pray for my neighbors. Although I have a strong inner faith, I don't classify myself as a charismatically religious person. I wasn't sure what exactly to pray for, but I knew that the current situation was unbearable for me and that something must change. So, I just simply prayed for help in loving my unlovable neighbors and for the relationship between us to improve.

Then, one day, my daughter ran in from playing outside and excitedly announced that she had the best news in the whole wide world. As I wondered what it could possibly be, the usual list of big deal events in my daughter's eyes ran through my head. Maybe the girls thought of a plan to all buy matching shoes at Target, or perhaps someone is having a birthday party at Club Libby Lu.

Before I could surmise a given scenario, she blurted out, "The Langleys are moving!!!"

As I tried to disguise the joy in my response, all I could think of to say was, "Wow, are you sure?"

"Yes, they are moving to Atlanta when school is over for her dad's new job," she said. They were the ringleaders of the meanies amongst us, and soon they would be gone!

Suddenly, that loving feeling toward my neighbors began to come back to me. I felt such relief that I could truly feel love for them again.

Even if I only really loved the fact that they were moving, it was still great to learn there would soon be a positive resolution around the corner.

Since my final tactic seemed to work so well, I decided to keep on praying. I prayed that nothing would delay their move. And, I also prayed for my incoming neighbors to be much easier to love than my outgoing ones. After all, it was not written to love your neighbors only when they deserve it, although that sure would have made it a lot easier for me to obey. So, I chalked this one up as a lesson learned for me and my kids…be kind, be nice, treat others as yourself, and turn it over to God for Him to work out. The meanies were moving, AMEN!

∼ The Wicked Stepmother *by Holly May* ∼

I always tell people that in my previous life, I "used" to be a nurse. I guess, technically, I am still a nurse; but that world is far, far away. I was very proud to become a nurse. I am the only person in my family to graduate from college, and I worked darn hard to do it. I was a divorced woman working two or three jobs to get through college. Then, I became a stepmother and everything changed.

I met my husband through work. I was the nurse, he was the doctor—terribly cliché, I know. He had three boys; I had made a solemn vow never to get involved with a man with children. Way too hard! We became friends and then fell in love. So much for solemn vows.

As a nurse, I was well respected and appreciated. As a stepmother, I am sometimes tolerated and often targeted. As a nurse, I often had glowing comments from patients posted for all to see. Patients and families showered me with cards and gifts. As a stepmother, there are LOTS of comments—none that I care to share! The "gifts" I receive come in the form of dirty laundry and dirtier dishes. My patients were elderly, feeble, and forgetful. My stepsons are teenage, sassy, and willful. Being a nurse was hard—life and death right there.

Being a stepmother is harder. It is all-consuming, thankless, and often painful.

Being a stepmother is the most educational thing I have ever done. I never wanted to be a stepmother. I have been mentally beaten more times than I care to count. These boys and I have been through it all, and I imagine we will continue to go through more as time goes on.

But, I can take it. I can take it because, while all of the above is true, I wouldn't trade my family for anything. None of us asked for this, but I believe that we are all better people for having experienced it. These boys, my boys, are smart, funny, wonderful, loving people. I know that I am truly a better person for knowing and loving them, and I hope that they can say the same.

As a nurse, I felt pride. As a stepmother, I feel amazing love for these three boys. I said that I never wanted to be a stepmother. Now, I wouldn't want to be anything else.

∼ Holiday Hullabaloo ∼
by Christine Louise Hohlbaum

When you leave the workplace to raise a family, something strange happens. Never mind the typical brain rot or extra poundage that frames your face. These things occur gradually as well. The most surprising thing to me was how incredibly insecure I became at being in public without my children. They were my auxiliaries, the little beings that clung to me, giving me shape and form, providing me with definition and a job to do. My level of incompetence at having a normal, adult conversation shocked me. If it didn't involve commands, warnings, and pointing fingers, I was at a loss as to what I should say. Words without exclamation points seemed as foreign to me as the clothing at which I was now staring.

Having received an invitation to my husband's office party, I struggled now to find something fitting to wear. I sucked in my belly and then let it out again. From the full-length mirror, I could see a bowlful of jelly jiggling back at me. I found a trendy skirt and brown fishbone top that barely covered me. Eying myself in the mirror, I was appalled to see how frizzy my hair looked. It hadn't been cut in eight months. I wrestled with my hair for a moment, realizing there was only one solution to my plight.

"Hairspray!" I whispered, soaking my locks with Aqua Net.

I am so uncool, I thought miserably, stuffing my feet into my not-made-for-Mommy shoes. I've never been catwalk material, but at least I used to have social grace. Years of ballet lessons taught me poise.

Peering at my opaque tummy in the dim light, I looked for that lithe ballerina amidst the lack of muscle definition in that area.

Just then, the doorbell rang. The baby-sitter arrived on time, which gave me four minutes to reapply my makeup before putting on my coat. My daughter inhaled loudly and exclaimed, "Mama! You are so chic!" This, coming from a four-year-old, was most flattering. She compared her stockings to mine and immediately asked if she could wear my skirt to preschool the following day. I smiled and spritzed my wrist with a bit of perfume. She didn't see my lumpy stomach or my wild hair. To her, I was Cinderella, transformed for an evening of mystery and adventure. To myself, I was not a stay-at-home mom. I was a goddess going out on the town.

My husband's office was celebrating the holidays in style at an Italian restaurant near their building. Having little occasion to venture far from my garden fence, I was pleased to leave my stain-resistant clothing at home, if only for one night.

Despite the early hour, it was already pitch-black outside. My children were concentrating on their licorice and barely waved me good-bye. That's not how a two-year-old should respond when his mother is leaving, I thought as I closed the front door behind me. They're getting older, I sighed, and clicked on the automatic car door opener. The cold winter air pressed against my bare skin.

The dimly lit restaurant added to my excitement. Right before I entered the eating area, I inhaled deeply, summoning the courage to present myself to my husband's colleagues. I had only met them once before at the company barbecue; but the children had been with us then, and I knew I had been invisible to most of them. Children have a way of Etch-A-Sketching all over a mother's existence so that she serves only as the backdrop to their presence.

Feeling naked in my fishbone blouse and tight-fitting skirt, I attempted to sashay into the room. My confidence plummeted when I saw I was one of the only spouses at the holiday dinner that evening. None of them had wanted to fight the evening traffic through Munich to attend the event. Not only did I not have my children to shield me from intimate cocktail conversation, but I was even more exposed by being the only non-company member at the event. My husband greeted me warmly and placed a glass of champagne in my hand.

Society dictates that if you want to make a good first impression, don't drink too much at the company holiday party. Having recently suffered the stomach flu, I still had a lowered tolerance for alcohol. Unfortunately, I noticed it a little too far into the evening.

The president of the company opened the buffet. He appeared rather stiff and a bit uncomfortable. I wondered if he really liked public speaking. We tried not to lunge toward the table with the silver serving plates and flickering flames. Instead, we decided to wait it out a while for the crowd to die down. We placed our drink order with a waiter who looked like Frodo from the Lord of the Rings. Since I was in a red wine mood and the night was still young, I ordered a glass. Several moments later, the waiter returned with an entire carafe of red wine just for me. I offered to share it with others, but there were no takers. I sipped my wine at first judiciously, then a bit more thirstily as the hunger pangs subsided. The room started to buzz a little strangely.

Just as we entered the buffet line, the chicken ran out. We waited for a good while, sipping some more of our wine and looking about us. I asked the waiter for a glass of water. He placed an entire bottle in front of my plate. Once the chicken was finally served, we each got just a smidgeon of food. The liquid-to-solid ratio looked a bit off-kilter. I toddled back to my chair.

At the time, it seemed like a good idea to stop after one helping. I even refused dessert, which is most uncharacteristic of me. Perhaps it was the ballooning belly I saw in the mirror a few hours earlier, or maybe it was the ringing in my brain. Suddenly, I noticed that the wine carafe was almost empty. How had that happened? I looked at my husband who was nursing his second apple juice.

"Schatz, you're driving home, right?" His eyes scrunched into a pleasant grin. His bout with the flu had come just days ago, so he was in no state to do what I had already done. We chatted with my husband's colleagues for another hour. I tried hard not to slur my words and soon gave up speaking altogether. With the wine gone, I gulped glass after glass of water, but to no avail. The light-headed sensation between my ears wouldn't go away.

When it was time to leave, I nudged my husband in the direction of the company president. With the sudden inspiration of the helplessly tipsy, I thought of a way out of my own embarrassment.

"You have to say thank you!" I demanded in a rather annoying, motherly voice. He glided over to him and shook his hand. In that moment, I do not know what overcame me. Instead of shaking the man's hand like any good German (which I am not), I gave him an old-fashioned American hug. He returned the favor with a bear hug that almost snapped the fishbone in my blouse. Both a little ruffled, we parted with smiles and a wave. He must have just appeared like a stiff man, I thought as my husband handed me my coat and hat. Pulling the beret snugly over my ears, I glanced in his direction again. On his table, in front of his plate, sat an empty wine carafe, too.

CHAPTER 6

MY CHILDREN KEEP ME LAUGHING AND CRYING

∼ **Negotiating 101** *by Mary Susan Buhner* ∼

Although I have my degree in communications, I prided myself (pre-motherhood) on taking several business classes from what we called "The B School" in college. My alma mater, Indiana University, has a nationally ranked "B School." For someone like me, who thrived on English literature and speech courses, signing up for the "Power of Negotiating" class was a bit intimidating. I was, however, confident that it would someday serve me well. And it did...until motherhood, the most challenging position of all.

Motherhood took all my textbook examples, role-playing, and negotiating tactics and dumped them right out the window. Along with it, tied to a cement block and a short rope, were my ego, composure, and sometimes dignity. For nothing, and I do mean nothing, prepared me for the complex negotiations, many of them nonverbal, that would take place between my children and me in the future.

In my former life, which I now affectionately refer to as "BK" (before kids), I worked in the not-for-profit sector as a major gifts fund-raiser. I loved my career, helping educational institutions raise funds for special projects and programs that benefited students of all ages. Over my tenure, the largest gift I negotiated was a $500,000 donation that we created as a matching dollar-for-dollar fund toward a Million Dollar Educational Endowment. My favorite gift ever received, however, is the least amount I ever raised. A quarter taped to a pledge card from a six-year-old boy named Danny. I was and still am a cause-driven person who loves the thrill of "closing the deal."

I prided myself on working for a Big Ten university, a private university, and a public school system, grades K-12, during my fundraising career. So when I was expecting my first child, I thought to myself, "No sweat!" Not only was I wrong about the no-sweat part, but also what I came to quickly realize is motherhood wasn't just sweat but rather, blood, sweat, and yes, tears! Lots of tears.

Eventually, I traded the conference room for the grocery store, my leather Coach briefcase for the grocery cart shaped like a miniature car solely for the amusement of my new clients, Susannah (age five) and Caroline (age two).

One day in particular I will never forget. While doing my weekly grocery shopping, it sank in. I might have had a "so-called" career premotherhood, but in the grocery store with kids in tow, none of what I learned in my college negotiating classes applied. I was on new ground here. No planning, no time to process or calculate my next move—only instincts and a little luck would get me through closing this deal.

It was a sunny Friday afternoon. I dropped my five-year-old daughter off at preschool, one of those half-day programs, which means two hours on a generous day. With limited time, I knew it would be easier to throw my groceries in the cart minus one child. Not to mention the hair pulling and screaming over whose free kiddy cookie from the bakery was bigger. Off I went with only my two-year-old in tow, my precious baby. Ah, it would be the proverbial piece of cake. With a smug smile on my face, I dreamed of getting in and out of the store today negotiation free. I banished from my mind my last failed negotiation over Barbie fruit snacks. No, today it would be in and out. That was my plan.

I confidently pulled out the grocery list from my purse/carry-on luggage-sized tote. All was going according to plan as my two-year-old daughter munched happily on her freebie cookie and waved to strangers. Getting cocky, I stopped at the salad dressing section to survey the new selections (or new to me, anyway). I thought perhaps today, I would actually take a minute and contemplate what I might enjoy eating. My mistake. The cart's halt obviously signaled to my daughter the okay to get out of the cart.

Cardinal Sin of grocery shopping that I momentarily forgot: NEVER LET YOUR KID(S) GET OUT OF THE CART! Once any child is out of the cart, it is war to stuff them back into the safety of the plastic car/cart.

I gasped aloud as I clutched my coveted bottle of Paul Newman's Raspberry Vinaigrette. Her chubby little leg swung over the side, in slow motion, as she readied herself. I know for a fact that I yelled aloud, "NOoooooooo!" as I dove toward her to stop the chaos. It was too late. She was out. The war was on!

I composed myself in one millisecond (what would be ten minutes for people in the "real" world). I gently set down the bottle of dressing in the cart, trying to act nonchalant about the situation. I looked around, calculating my options. Bribery? Nope. Cookie is already in hand. Yelling? Not working. Spanking? We don't do that. Staring war? Maybe.

I made my move. After all, they teach you in negotiating classes that the best defense is to play offense. I might have even let out a cheery whistle as if to emphasize my control over the matter. Little did my toddler know that I had sweat dripping down my rib cage, and my heart was about to explode. I had a basket full of groceries; I had to check out in the next 15 minutes to pick my oldest daughter up from school—I had a lot at stake here!

I calmly started to walk toward her as she laughed and squealed with delight. Sensing my hidden urgency and with the speed of a jackrabbit, she darted to the front of the cart. There I was in aisle 16A, faced off with a two-year-old, so far losing the negotiation of my life.

I growled calmly and sternly, "Caroline, get in the little car, honey." She smiled big and scrunched up her nose and confidently reported back to me, "No! I am staying out!"

Negotiations got ugly. Nothing I proposed worked. We needed a compromise, but not without one last power move. Instincts took over, and I began to grab for her. She took off around the cart, and before I knew it, I was chasing my two-year-old in a circle around the stupid red car/cart, whatever you call it. I could not reach her, and I could not catch her. Reason with a two-year-old? Huh, I dare you! With minutes to go, I knew I didn't have time for a full-out, drop yourself on the floor, terrible two's tantrum, and I was not leaving my grocery cart only to have to come back and possibly face the same fate twice.

So I gave it the old college try one last time and tried to sprint around the cart to nab her. It was then, without any words, my two-year-old and I "closed the deal" and negotiated our final terms with each other in one clear but nonverbal exchange. We would agree to disagree, but we would work together, each giving a little bit to the other.

As I made my final lap around the cart, she brilliantly threw herself on the front hood of the plastic car attached to my completely full grocery cart. Her little knuckles were white with determination, indicating with confidence that she was not letting go anytime this century. I slowly stretched my neck from side to side and resumed pushing the cart. I am fully aware that I looked like an idiot as I strolled to the checkout line with a toddler hanging white-knuckled to the front of the cart. Caroline remained outside the car; I finished my grocery shopping. I smiled at the horrified 16-year-old cashier, wiped the sweat from my brow, and sighed, knowing that I might not have won this one textbook style, but I did close the deal!

~ **Y.A. Y.A.** *by Leslie Fleischman* ~

At the ripe and fertile age of 30, I lived in the city, had a full-time, semi-rewarding, creative marketing job for a cosmetics giant, and a fun and loving husband. More than anything, I wanted to put my virtual maternal instinct into reality mode. After two years of marriage and not having to "try" too hard, I became proudly pregnant. I was certain that I would be a delightful mom. On a glorious spring day, my first daughter was born. With just enough time to take the best shower I have ever had in my life, I was released from the hospital. I nursed and pumped, pumped and nursed, and slept a little. Let the coffee flow and motherhood begin.

The fresh breath of spring had barely turned into a sweaty summer in the city, and my maternity leave was over, and—ugh, I still had a job. Checked off the list of interview questions, weighed my options, and left my little girl with a stranger who liked to sing Jamaican folk songs. When I arrived home, I was usually a bit exhausted but happy to have my blue-green-eyed, soft-haired little girl all to myself to feed and play with. My day was complete the minute the nanny closed the door behind her. No matter what corporate stresses came my way, that baby reminded me instantly what was important in my life. And as my superiors noticed, my priority was no longer work. The baby's needs were simple and pure, and I made her so happy. She didn't give me a review or care if my clothes were "fabulous." Just love, love, love, occasional sleep deprivation, and spit-up on my shoulder.

Every moment was teachable and touchable and singable. I was light-hearted and enchanted. The second baby came along, equally as splendid, and the two girls together could take my breath away. I petitioned my husband to support my decision to stop working a full-time job. I was desperate, it seems, to have the life of a desperate housewife. My good cheer and loyalty kept me on the corporate payroll for a job I could do from home. Perfect! I was the stay-at-home mom I had always wanted to be. I called the shots, master of my own agenda.

No longer needing to be minutes from the office, we turned our attention to the 'burbs. We were now part of the urban migration to the house, the yard, new furnaces, good public schools, bad takeout food, and lots of driving. Pretty soon, my baby girl was walking, and my oldest was talking full throttle. Baby number three was on the way. My son was born—an extraordinary, solid, beautiful, healthy child. For the first several months, I was bending over backwards to ensure that the girls were adjusting to having a brother.

And then I started to yell. As the months moved on, so did my yelling. I was starring in my own scary movie. My mouth opened, and vile passion rushed out. When I yelled, it was like a mole coming out from under the fresh, pristine, spring grass. It was staggering and furry and downright gross. I never dreamed that I would yell with such rage. I know what it feels like to be yelled at and to listen to yelling, and I hadn't liked it one bit.

Due to the abundance of yelling in my own youth, I spent a good part of my childhood confused, frustrated, and unnerved. I was never really sure when Mt. Miriam, my mom, would blow. How could she treat her own precious daughter, me, like that? And if she wasn't getting angry with me, the supermarket clerk would do just fine, which rendered its own form of dreadfulness. With all that yelling in my memory banks, I swore that when I was a mom, I would embody sugar and spice and everything nice.

It didn't take too long to recognize that the addiction to yelling was now a part of me, and it had become part of my life again. When I yelled and saw their little heads snap around, their shoulders tighten up, and their eyes widen with surprise, I felt myself heading toward "rock bottom." I needed to recover my sanity, my center, and their feelings of security. I am absolutely not suggesting that anyone raising children should be refused the right to yell once in a while. That would be the equivalent of saying a mom is actually *not* entitled to be alone in the bathroom until her children are grown. After all, we are human and often called upon to be superhuman.

While at a party, I came across a woman, Jane, who included me, a practical stranger, in her cathartic conversation. Aside from both having three children, we seemed very different. Jane, rather colorless, wears button-down shirts, almost all buttoned up, and throws candle parties on a Tuesday evening, a "plain Jane" if you will. I show cleavage, wear makeup, turn my house into a dance club, and just learned to surf. To be neighborly, I welcomed her back to town after her family had relocated to Chicago and back again.

With the negative spin I always associated her with, she let me know that she was finding the chore of getting settled in difficult. "All I do is scream and yell. The truth is," she told me, "I yell all the time. I've always yelled. It's horrible." Alas, her confessions pointed out that we weren't completely different after all. That was the beginning of "Yellers Anonymous," and Jane became an official member of the unofficial recovery program, Y.A., Y.A.—not to be confused with "Blah, Blah Anonymous," which is recovery for those who can't help but keep you occupied as they bore you incessantly about the endless string of carpools that they have to drive, unplanned doctors visits, and what they need at the grocery store. Not to mention indecision over paint color choices.

No wonder we sometimes scream. Our days are filled with so much of this random chatter from those around us, big and small. But we don't yell at our friends for annoying us. We yell at our unsuspecting children. Yelling at our partners in front of our children—just as bad. Occasionally yelling at a customer service agent—excusable. Some of us yell in front of our doors, others behind closed doors.

Our children, in their effort to soak up what life is, copy many of the moves we make. So it shouldn't come as a surprise when the day arrives that they begin to yell back. Then comes the ultimate hypocritical scenario, when you find yourself saying, "IF YOU YELL AT ME ONE MORE TIME...!" or "YOU CANNOT SPEAK TO ME THAT WAY, YOU...!" Do we even notice the irony? A parenting transgression played out often in different ways. "Do as I say, not as I do" doesn't seem to work. Sort of like drinking diet soda while lobbying for the healthy benefits of milk and water.

Yelling, in my case, has been passed down from generation to generation like holiday dinners and procrastination. And now, along with singing, manners, and blond hair, I passed on yelling, too. While in first grade, my middle child had made a nice, quiet friend. She always wanted to call this child for a play date. But after the first two play dates, I got only excuses from the other mom. Never a "well, can't this week, how about next?" So, eventually I gave up. A year or so later, the play date boycott was explained. It seems that my daughter screamed at her friend on their last play date. The friend didn't like it. At first I thought, oh come on, welcome to the world, little play date boycotter. But then I realized, no, welcome to our world. It was at that moment I wished I could have taken it all back. Do over!

When a yelling tirade is finished, we are left stressed, sore-throated (if you are loud enough), guilt-ridden, and surrounded by a noxious form of bad energy rather like the underlying odor left lingering by cigarette smoke. Extreme yelling is a dangerous sport, and I knew I had to get off the circuit. I went on a journey to figure out why I yelled. In the end, I worked through some issues I didn't know I had, and learned to recognize learned behaviors.

Ultimately, self-control, softer substitutes, and meaning what I said, the first time, were essential to overcoming my bad behavior. So I tried a couple of new techniques, like whispering. At the dinner table, on any given evening, my kids wouldn't stay seated for more than 45 seconds until they had to get up and do something. Of course, I told them approximately two times each, for a total of six times in 11 minutes, to stay in their chairs.

Just when the last kid got up anyway and I was about to blow my stack, I re-grouped and said, "Pssst, I have something to tell you guys." They all three cocked their heads to hear my secret. What I said was, "If anyone gets up again, I'm going to assume you are finished and take your food away, and the kitchen will be closed." They giggled, and they listened. More importantly, the three former American Olympian jumping beans finished up their dinners, cleared their plates, and went on their way—after they were excused. My throat wasn't sore, my stomach was knot-free, and nobody cried and looked at me like I was a freak with ten shrieking heads.

Not yelling requires concentration, self-awareness, noticing the warning signs, and being well-rested and alcohol-free. If all those criteria are not in alignment, along with the planets and the tide, a deep breath and remembering that you asked for these kids may help. Unquestionably, practice makes better.

Not yelling has changed me and changed our lives. We laugh more, listen more, speak nicely to each other, and we actually do "feel the love." We all feel a little disillusioned when any of us returns to our old ways. At least now, we know the unmitigated difference between being human and being a human out of control. If I maintain a consistent record, perhaps my children will not have to wonder on the "couch" how I could yell at them with such ferocity.

For the luck of longevity, I have had the pleasure of my parents mellowing. I have witnessed the decline of their earsplitting ways. In spite of their yelling and screaming and some unfortunate name-calling, I loved them, a lot. For posterity, I interviewed my parents on videotape. I recently watched that interview.

There was one question and answer that jumped out at me, slapped me in the face, and patted me on the back. "If you could change one thing about how you parented," I asked, "what would that be?"

They thought for a few seconds, gazing into our history, shifted in their seats, and looking back into the camera, they agreed that they would have changed—"nothing." As our enlightened generation knows, the first step to recovery is admitting you have the problem.

"My name is Leslie Fleischman, and I am a yeller." If you're interested in obtaining further information about "Yellers Anonymous," well, just give a holler!

∼ A Really Crappy Day *by Michelle Stiles* ∼

I have four daughters, ages three, two, and my twins are almost one. We are trying to potty train our two-year-old Mackenzie. Hailey is our three-year-old, and Sophie and Savannah are our twins.

One day, while I was in the shower, Mackenzie came in and said that she had to poop. She climbed up on the "big girl potty," so I thought she went successfully in the toilet. The next thing I knew, the twins came crawling into the bathroom, and Savannah was covered in poop. She had it all over her face, squished between her fingers, and all over her clothes. Poop was smeared from the dining room, through the kitchen, and into the bathroom.

I jumped out of the shower to get Savannah cleaned up first. Then, I had to clean the floor so the babies didn't get into it again. Mackenzie had, indeed, flushed the toilet, but only after she had stuffed a whole roll of toilet paper in, causing it to overflow all the way into the kitchen! I immediately threw down towels to try and soak up the mess. I called my husband, asking him to come home to help fix the toilet. He had just dropped off Hailey at preschool. I had everything cleaned up and was giving the twins a bath when he returned home. All that was left for him to do was to fix the toilet, while I continued to watch my kids, plus three others that I care for. This gives a whole new meaning to having a really "crappy" day!

∾ How NEW Is New? *by Joy J. Bunville* ∾

As I ponder on what it has meant to be a full-time stay-at-home mother, I must reflect on the times when my own mother would tell me during an argument or little attitudinal tuff (since I always wanted to have my own way): "You're going to wish you were this age again in your lifetime, and I hope I am around to see it!" At least once a week, it seemed, my mother would remind me of this prediction. Yes, maybe I was head-strong growing up, but I never once thought about ever reverting back to those God awful pre-teen, teenage, and college years.

I am the mother of one simply gorgeous, unique, jovial, bubbly, the-apple-of-my-eye, incredibly smart, brilliant, radiantly daunting, entrancing little girl named Samantha. She is my life. Everything I do is for her; every breath I breathe is for her because she needs me. Every Advil pain reliever I take so that I can continue my day is for her alone. Every cup of coffee I brew (and I double the grounds in the filter to make it extra strong) is for her so I can tackle each day. Every time I bathe my butt, put on clean underwear (maybe not a bra), and place the top clothing layer on (this top layer is usually a day or two worn) is for her. And every time I place money in my wallet and the money is spent on Samantha, as far as gas, clothing, food, medicine, niceties—it's because I love my "Honey Bunny" endlessly!

During the era when my mother was mothering (mind you, my mother is 60, and I am 31), women were earning a living and raising their families. My mom graduated college, became a registered nurse, married, had children, then divorced and continued to rear three, four-year accredited college-educated children. Norene would always say to me that I can do what I put my mind to: Well, I am an artist, I love to read and live life, I am married, I have one child, and I stay at home full-time, and this was not in my mother's plans for any of her children. Sometimes I know that my mother looks at me with disbelief because, although Samantha is an incredible little woman, my mom wants to know, "What are you going to do with your life?" This seems like an unfair question.

My life is for my daughter. Yes, my husband gets on my nerves sometimes. Yes, I wish I made full-time money on a job somewhere. Yes, I want a new car. Yes, I do not want to have to move back home with my mother during the pivotal points in my life with my daughter, and still married. But, I am first and foremost my daughter's mother. I am Samantha's soothsayer when she needs my shoulders to cry on; I am the one to reassure her that she is right with the world, regardless of all that surrounds her! I always hope to be the one she turns to when she is blue-at-the-mouth and feels put upon.

I do not want my daughter feeling as if she cannot come and tell Mommy. I grew up feeling like I could not tell Mommy because she was working, she was tired, and she would get angry and be unfair. I want to keep as level a head as possible in this life with my Honey Bunny.

Life teaches us unbelievable lessons. When my life was only about me, nothing was off-limits. My husband and I would venture to new heights— new cities to live, new dwelling places to reside, think about new careers and then take them on. Now we try to stay constant—as long as the money is constant and the health benefits are stable, we are good.

After giving birth to Samantha and being released from the hospital, I stayed at my mother's home for a month to gather my strength back. I remember being exhausted, my breasts were killing me, my vagina hurt like hell, I was thirsty, I walked slow, I wore my eyeglasses every day, and I wore a big-mama smock as a nightgown because I was breast-feeding constantly—you know, I was in a pseudo-me state.

Samantha began crying constantly after about the second day for some strange reason—seriously, the only time she did not cry was when she was on the breast—then that was not enough.

My mother had advice for me: "Give her some water." My doctor told me NO water for the first year of my daughter's life. My mother had more advice for me: "Feed her." All I could think of was: What the hell else can I do, because I have tried that, and I have held Samantha, and now I am at the point of complete delirium?

My husband thought he would pick her up and sneak away and give her water. I damn near had a fit. This man knows what the doctor told me because I told him. But to his benefit, so that the hen keeper did not arise in me, I took my baby from him because I knew he was at a loss, too.

Imagine me: The new mother with a green, white, and pink-spotted big-mama muumuu on, with my hair in braids that were drawn in a ponytail on the crown of my head. I felt as if I could barely see—the blur before my eyes was so intense through my black, sleek-trimmed glasses. I wore black pregnancy panties that held my belly securely (one size fits all) with one of the huge pads that the hospital gives you because you secrete juices for days; and my breasts would not stop leaking, so I had a wet chest—and the people closest to me had everything to say, and it sounded like ABSOLUTELY NOTHING.

This one particular night, Samantha would not be quiet, and it was like two or three in the morning. I turned on my night-light again, and I picked her up above my head, and I shook her a little, and I cried aloud and said: "WHAT DO YOU WANT FROM ME?"

She cried louder. I only slightly shook her, and I freaked. I then realized that my daughter only wants what is rightfully hers—HER MOTHER AT ALL COSTS. Regardless of sleep deprivation, colds, aches, and money, my daughter needs me to be the mommy that Samantha was birthed to make me.

Life changes you. Being at home and chronicling every time that my daughter laughed, crawled, and walked; when she used the potty first (the pee and poop); when she grew each tooth; when she began saying words, then sentences, then stating that she was going to Harvard; when she ate a vegetable; when she got her first twin big-girl bed, and the rhinoceros was trying to get her—these are moments in time I will never trade for a dollar.

My mother was right. I do wish I were this age again, because these years are blissful, and I will never wish I did anything different in being at home with my Samantha full-time during her formative years. My life as a full-time mother is priceless!!

So, I suppose being a full-time mother now and being a full-time mother during the fifties, sixties, and seventies may not be so different. The money is still green—the equivalency is simply different; you need more now than then, but the level of sacrifice is the same. The toys are the same as before; they just have cooler colors and names. We mothers take lots of pictures, scribble lots of keepsake notes, and coo and caw about our children. And as I look at my mother, Samantha's grandmother, I know that being a mother now is truly a recycled version of what it was—it's just that fads are different, and now everything is online and on the cell phone, and both online and cell phones are in the trains, planes, and automobiles.

∼ Escape to Toilet Land ∼
by Christine Velez-Botthof

I'll never forget one of my first interview experiences. I was seated in the president's office of a mega-magazine publishing house in New York City. I was excited to be there. In fact, I was more than excited. The job was on the table: Executive Assistant to the President. Did I want it? Could I handle it? What was I made of? How much sleep did I require for an above average performance? All questions in front of me...all answers that came easily. Yes, I wanted the job. Yes, of course, I could handle it! I was made of steel. A just barely beyond adolescent machine, ready to bite, push, and shove my way to the top, even if it meant I'd have to crawl. Sleep? "Who needs sleep," I remember saying. I was 22 years old and a night owl, to say the least. I could go all day and all night and all day again with very little sleep to speak of.

Just as I was about to rally yahoo in honor of my new job, there was a pause in my interview, and I was informed of something crucial. It seemed the assistant at the time, the one I was to replace, could oftentimes be found in the ladies' room, bawling her eyes out, usually over something my prospective boss said to her in the heat of a deadline and, more often than not, in front of a room full of people.

I was then asked whether or not I'd be willing to undergo such emotional rigors for the benefit of a paycheck, and not a very big one at that. I was not.

Yet here I am, over a decade later, locked in the bathroom, crying my eyes out.

Not because the president of some magazine just yelled at me but because my nine-month-old is in the other room, screaming his head off when he should be napping, and I haven't a clue how to get him to stop.

I haven't showered, brushed my teeth, or even dressed yet, and it's well past noon. The closest thing I've had to food all day has been a biter biscuit hurled at my head and a spoonful of oatmeal and bananas tossed onto my pajamas.

Noon means nap. But my little bundle of rambunctious joy doesn't seem to agree today. And not yesterday or the day before that, either. Yet I try. I try to get him to go down, just for a moment of peace. A moment I find myself praying for.

"Please God, I'll use the spare time to wash baby bottles and vacuum the floor, please, if you just grant me this one nap, I won't be too selfish with the space."

My son woke up screaming at two a.m. and stayed that way until way past five a.m. Nothing I did seemed to soothe him. No acceptable lullabies or amount of rocking could get him to stop. It was another loooong night. Shouldn't he be exhausted and, like me, craving this time to be alone, in his room, to catch up on sleep? It seems the only thing he's craving right now is for Mommy to pick him up, and Mommy just can't because she's sitting on the toilet, waiting for someone to come in and pick her up. I'm beyond exhausted, hungry, frustrated, and, above all, alone. He's out there, and I'm in here, and it's times like these when I wonder how it all came to this. I am not getting paid for these tears—they're free. I am a stay-at-home mom.

I never took that magazine job. But I took others. Lots of them. I became a journalist. My first opportunity was in Birmingham, Alabama, and that led to several jobs in several states up and down the Northeastern seaboard. I worked a lot, traveled a lot, and in a six-year span managed to move at least seven times. All for the sake of my career.

I started out low and worked my way up, until I landed a gig in New York City as a newsroom assignment manager. I sat in what would be considered the "epicenter" of the newsroom. Every story of the day passed my desk before it did anything else. I cooked every idea for almost every story. Research—me. Story set-up—me again. New stories, old stories, good stories, bad stories, health, wealth, blood, sweat, tears—all me. I managed several field crews, reporters, producers, and interns, all at once. When a story fell through, it was my job to find another one. When a story broke, it was my job to staff it...only after I was sure it was worth chasing after. I stroked egos and soothed dreams. I took a lot of grief and gave it all right back. My job was ruthless and not for the meek at heart. I worked ten hours a day, and it was never enough.

I followed *The New York Times, The Daily News*, MSNBC, CNBC, Bloomberg, Reuters, *The Washington Post, The Miami Herald,* The Associated Press, the NYPD, FDNY, the mayor, the White House, the Pentagon, the Pope, the Nikkei, and currencies from 20 other foreign countries—and that was just the first cup of coffee.

Amid the disastrous headlines and my daily recital of a popular news anthem, "if it bleeds it leads," I always managed to ponder world peace. A place of quiet solitude where skyscrapers would be replaced with rolling hills, and flowers would bloom where subway grates once stood. I dreamt of a place where a child's laughter could be heard for miles, washing out the grunt of the corporate world.

The more I fantasized about this imaginary place, the closer I was to becoming a mom. I thought moving away from the pace of New York City and back to a place like Birmingham, where my then fiancé lived, would be the answer. It was the kids laughing and playing, those versions of the dream that inched me across miles of my life's work and back down the countryside, to a place I now call home.

No more Bloomberg, no more *New York Times*, no more subways, no more AP. These days I read *Parents, Parenting*, BabyZone.com, *American Baby, Baby Style* (yes, that exists!), *Goodnight Moon, Hello Baby*, and basically anything with some sort of fuzzy animal, colorful number, or furry letter on the front cover. If it chirps, moos, meows, barks, or quack quacks, I'm on it.

I don't get far into any of these books, magazines, or toys. My son won't hear of it. He has an attention span that's just slightly larger than my husband's but shorter than, say, the word "ouch."

Quite frankly, I seem to have a hard time keeping up with anything these days. I barely speak in complete sentences anymore and certainly not one that doesn't involve the use of some sort of rhyme scheme. "The baby-waby doesn't like the bookie-wookie?" It's an irritating habit and one that may require some sort of patch to get rid of. For now, I use it to soothe myself (mommy-wommy on the toilet-woilet because baby-waby is crying) and drive everyone else around me away. Not a good thing. I've been hung up on because of it.

Those are just a couple of new habits I have taken on. Like my son's temperament, they are ever changing, like a revolving door of techniques for mommy survival.

Today, survival for me is sitting here on this toilet, while he wails in his crib. We both want to be held, yet, maybe not by each other right now. One of the things I never realized about motherhood is the fact that your child really can, and will, get sick of you. Just like you might tire of him and his nonstop crying, non-sleeping, constant diaper changing, picky-eating self. In times like these, if you don't have a new trick up your sleeve, you're left to your own devices to try and figure out how to entertain a brain that is just slightly larger than a Ping-Pong ball and does not want to nap so you can conjure up something new to delight and amaze.

In my old life, entertainment came easily. I worked hard, and I played hard. I got dressed up, I went out. I dressed down and went to ball games; I went to the movies and out to dinner. I went to parties and museums and parties at museums. I was, at one time, considered social and—dare I say—fashionable. I was always late to things, because I could be.

As a mom, I am never, ever late—for anything. I never oversleep, because, rewind 15 years, I never get any sleep. In the haze of sheer exhaustion, I have been known to wash my face with Listerine instead of Sea Breeze and pour breast milk into my cereal bowl. These days, my idea of fashion is a clearance center T-shirt for $2.99. One that can withstand flying foods and other human excretions I don't care to mention. I am a sweatpants wearer, and I can't say I mind. I have traded in my Jimmy Choos for a pair of sandals made by a man named Coconut. They don't have a heel, and they don't make a fuss. They're just sandals, and they fit. I chase my son in them. I don't go to the movies anymore and haven't a clue what I'd do with myself in a grown-up situation, alone, without baby. We're a team, he and I. And even though this team's currently in time-out, I'm always on his side. I love him and the sport of being his mom. Hanging up my dancing shoes has been little sacrifice. These days, I dance barefoot in the grass with my baby.

I've traded in my chopsticks for little spoons with plastic tops. No more sushi and sake. Instead, I play food games like "open the door" when my son puts on his picky-eater face and seals his lips so tight, Houdini couldn't slide a piece of rice paper through them. I've given up fancy handbags for the trusty, no-name baby bag. I don't wear lipstick so I can play "kissy kissy" with my boy all day. He loves it, it makes him laugh, and it makes us laugh. It's that laugh, that tiny little giggle that keeps me going, because no matter what, I know it's always in there, and it's my job to get it out. Not like getting your boss mad at you and trying to make it up. You can't tickle your boss all over his (or her) tummy until he bursts into hysterics, now can you?

Instead of driving home from work every afternoon, we drive to the park. And even though there is no five o'clock bell for moms, I can honestly say, I wouldn't turn off the hours I spend with my little man, crying or not. Sure he can be difficult, but so can I. He puts up with me, and I put up with him. My life without him was always filled with dreams of him.

And now he's here. He's the vision I've always had. That dream of peace in my world. It's like some magical karma boomeranged itself into my life, propelled me into motherhood, and made every single silly cliché a consistent reality for me. I have known this child since I myself was a little girl. The smile that spreads across his face when he sees me is enough to transform this once ruthless journalist into a big giant ball of mush.

I know there is some type of stereotype out there about stay-at-home mothers, although I'm not quite sure what it is and if it even warrants any merit. I work harder and longer than my hardest and longest job (and believe me—that is A LOT). I don't get a rest (except for this here bathroom break), and I don't get a vacation from being a mom. And I don't want one. This is my job now, and it pays more in rewards than any full-time corporate job ever will. I have nothing to prove, and that is, by far, the greatest relief of all. As far as I'm concerned, I've traded up. My position is higher than the greatest of titles, because I am the universe to a very little soul. It's a lot to live up to, but I'm up for the challenge. A little older and a little wiser and, luckily, supported by a wonderful husband and father.

And there you have it. Mommy survival at its best. I've managed to talk myself off this ledge. In answer, the way it all came to this is simple: Love. So, I'm going to unlock this bathroom door and let the corporate world do without me. For now, I'm going to go rock my baby, because like they say down south, "Babies don't keep."

∼ "My Mommy Uses Bad Words" ∼
by Julianne Rettig

This week marks the fifth anniversary of my official status as a stay-at-home mom. I have been home just long enough for my husband to forget that my nearly 20 years of hard work laid the foundation for all we now have and that we could not have made it this far without my help at the start. I have also been home just long enough for me to wonder whether I have any marketable skills.

The other day, my two-year-old son told me that I needed to get a job. I asked him what he thought I should do, and he told me, "Cleaning, washing..." That's great. College degree, two decades in the workplace, four decades on this planet, and I am now fit to be a housekeeper, and a lousy one at that, if you ask my husband.

While I have forfeited my hopes of pursuing a career (or anything else for that matter) to stay at home to educate and nurture my children, they credit their father for all of their knowledge and skills. If I hear, "Well, Daddy told me..." one more time, I think my head will explode.

Wait, I did get credit for something. During story time at my five-year-old daughter's school, they were discussing good words and bad words. My daughter quickly raised her hand and informed her teachers and classmates that "My mommy uses bad words." I cried for two days. I do recall saying "crap" one time and telling her that it is a bad word and that she should not repeat it. Motherhood Lesson #12,896—Do not call attention to your faults; they WILL be used against you.

So, now I sit, staring down the barrel of the big 4-0, wondering what to do with my life. My son will start preschool soon, and then I will have to seek gainful employment. So, what will a 40-something woman who has not worked in seven or so years do? Go back to the same unfulfilling career I had before children? Start a new career? Attend graduate school? My husband turns green at the thought of several more years of no income and more outflow of money.

I know that when I do start back to work, there will still be bathing, clothing, and feeding to attend to. The laundry will still need laundering. There will be homework and housework, and I would venture to guess that I will be the one doing it.

But, as much as I feel overwhelmed and unappreciated at times, I do love being there for my family. I have actually started cooking again—and enjoying it. I would miss not taking my children to school and not picking them up and looking through their school folders and hearing about their day.

I tell myself to stay in the moment and stop worrying about what will be tomorrow and what was yesterday. But, I am a planner and a worrier. And, if all that has happened in one's life shapes who we are today, I understand why I am such a twisted lump of clay. I can't help obsessing about my children's future, all while hearing the echo of my mother's voice, "You'll see...when *you* are a mother."

As a mother, I have been reduced to tears of sorrow and lifted to tears of joy. I have made my children laugh so hard they cry. I have made them cry so hard they laugh. No one can break your heart—or mend your heart—quite like your child can.

I know that I would not have made it this far without the help, support, and constant advice of close friends who ventured into motherhood before me. They have helped me see the humor in an otherwise crazy world and let me know that I am not alone in this journey.

It has taken me a while to accept my new status, but overall, I have grown quite comfortable with being a stay-at-home mom...finally, when it all may rapidly be coming to a close. So, today, I will live in the moment and enjoy every second, because it does go by so quickly. I will sit with my son and watch "Blue's Clues" or play Barbie with my daughter, even though I know that there are at least a thousand other things I "need" to be doing. Because I have come to the conclusion that we can do it all, but we cannot do it all well.

CHAPTER 7

BACK TO BRINGING HOME THE BACON

∼ The Most Stressful Position in the World ∼
by Theresa Joyce

I have been in the workforce for 20 years. I have always had a stressful position and used to think I could handle anything. That was until I had children.

In my opinion, the most stressful position in the world is being a stay-at-home mom. I had my first child just before my 31st birthday, and after the first six weeks of his birth, I decided to go back to work. (Little did I know how smart that was.) Two years later, my second child was born, and my husband and I had already made the decision for me to go back to work. Our second child was barely six months old when I became pregnant with the third. My husband and I discussed the possibility of me staying home, but that became quickly squashed when I received a promotion at work.

After two years in this new position, I started to feel like I was ready to stay home and raise my children. I thought, "How hard could it be?" I know lots of women who stay home, and they love it. (I did not realize that they were lying; well, most of them were.) I used to make comments like, "My house will be spotless," "I will have a schedule for the girls to do artwork and learn their letters and numbers," "We will go to the park two days a week, and I will work out," "Dinner will be ready every night at six, and the laundry will never pile up again." Wow, that would be great. Man, little did I know what was in store for me.

Anyway, without making the choice myself, I was dismissed at my job at the beginning of this year. What a break—not only do I get to stay home, but I will be able to collect unemployment at the same time.

For the first two months, I kept my children in childcare so I could get the house in order. I painted the outside, reorganized the garage, bedroom closets, and kitchen cabinets. By the beginning of March, I was ready for the kids to stay home full-time. The first week was a lot of fun. I spent all day playing with the kids. I thought, this is easy, until I realized that the house was a wreck, no laundry had been done, and the newly organized kids' rooms looked like a tornado had gone through them. So I had to come up with some kind of schedule.

I had it all worked out; while the girls are eating breakfast, I will start the laundry and clean the kitchen. I had no idea that as soon as I left the room, the girls were going to find other things to entertain them. They did things like dump out all 36 puzzles into one big pile; crumble their food into small micro pieces and throw it all over the living room; drag out every piece of clothing from their dressers and strew them through-out the rooms. I was only out of sight for ten minutes. I spent the rest of the day putting everything back and vacuuming.

The next day, I locked up the bedrooms and put up all the puzzles and did not start the housework until they were finished eating. I put in a video, and both of them (my oldest is in school now) sat down on the couch and looked as if they were going to be there a while. I put a load of laundry in the washer and started cleaning the kitchen. Maybe five minutes had passed; I poked my head around the corner to check on them. "Damn, where did they go?" They were in the bathroom, taking the small rinse cups, dipping them into the toilet, and pouring the water onto the floor.

I was speechless. I just dried them and the floor and proceeded to put them back into the living room with such protest from them, I had to think fast. "Oh, I know; do you two want to color?" I received huge grins and squeals that would have shattered glass. I settled them at the coffee table with all their coloring books (about 40) and crayons (about 100). Yeah, yeah, yeah, I know, big mistake.

Everything went great for about ten minutes when, once again, they disappeared. I guess at some point I had unlocked their bedroom door, because that is where I found them, making beautiful artwork on their closet doors and on the white Berber carpet. So, without giving you a day-to-day account of things they did, I will just list a few more things they have done over the last two months:

Take toothpaste and smear it all over the walls

Take an entire roll of toilet paper and put in the toilet

Take an entire roll of toilet paper and shred it into a million pieces

The four-year-old decided to stand over the two-year-old's pillow and pee on it

Empty the shampoo bottle onto the bathroom floor

Make designs on the couch with the yogurt

Stuff Play-Doh in every crack of the play radio

Color each other with markers (thank God they were washable)

Take a bag of chips and stomp on them and then pour orange juice over them

Well, now we spend most of the day at the mall or at the park, and I don't clean until the nighttime, just like before when I had a "paying" job. And soon, they start summer camp three days a week for four hours a day. Maybe then I will enjoy staying home. But for now, if you know of anyone hiring, please give him or her my number!

∼ The Mother of All Careers ∼
by Liz Rabiner Lippoff

I was finishing up my senior year in college when I interviewed for my first teaching job. The interviewer was a junior high principal from "The Hot District," where everyone wanted to work. I thought the interview was a disaster. I tried my hardest to be cool, calm, and professional, but he seemed intent on rattling me. Finally, he asked the question he'd been saving. "Do you plan on teaching for a long time?"

I had always wanted to teach, would have paid HIM to let me teach. But the interview had degenerated beyond repair, or so I thought, and I snapped, "Are you asking if I'm going to quit and have babies? Because, family or no family, I will always be a teacher." I probably didn't storm off in a huff, but that's how I remember it now, more than 30 years later. When the call came from that same district, I was floored.

"Miss Rabiner, one of our principals wants to offer you a job, but we can't seem to find your paperwork." The crumpled, soiled application was on the floor of the car, but I ironed it and filled it out. It was the principal/interviewer who hired me.

"I don't want teachers who are going to bitch in the faculty lounge," he explained. "I want people who will give it to me straight."

Ironically, he had asked the right question after all. I loved teaching, but four years later, I had a complete change of heart. I met my husband at the end of my first year of teaching, married him within 11 months, took a leave of absence two years later to have our first daughter...and never went back to full-time teaching. Several years earlier, when a friend had quit a terrific job to stay at home with her kids, I had been aghast at her explanation, but it became my own as well: I'd rather look back in 20 years and say, "I blew it on my career" than say, "I blew it on my kids."

My husband and I made a deal that may not seem very modern to some, but it suited both of us and still does. He was born to be a daddy, but he loved his job, a high-profile, high-stress career that invariably meant a move every few years. I tried being a full-time teacher and a mommy at the same time, but I was conflicted at work, the house wasn't running the way I liked it, and our babysitter was seeing our kids more than I was...and making more money to boot.

While I never loved housecleaning, I did love everything else about being a stay-at-home mommy. Our deal: He would pay the rent, so to speak, and I would be in charge of the kids, the house...and the moves. He could be the 100 percent daddy he wanted to be, when he wasn't at work. I could, in theory, be a corporate executive or sit around the house eating bonbons, as long as I handled the home front. As it turns out, I was mostly a wife and mommy, partly a volunteer, occasionally a working girl, and, plenty of times, an independent chick at the gym or the track. I had my cake and could eat it, too, but I'm not kidding myself. I couldn't have done it without a husband who liked the very same cake.

We moved half a dozen times. For several years, I did some substituting and an occasional part-time gig, but it couldn't compare to having my own classes, and I no longer wanted that. I craved something stimulating and satisfying "on the side," but it would have to be something very flexible. Even when the kids were out of grade school, into competitive swimming, and very busy, I liked my time at home, and

I liked being available for my family. An added incentive as the kids became teenagers: I wanted to be home on and off, unpredictably, in fact, so that the kids would never know when I might walk in the door.

I never really had a concrete plan, although, since it turned out so well for all of us, I'd like to claim credit. The truth is, I made each choice as it came up. When the girls were three and five and we lived in the Bay Area, I answered an ad for a part-time, temporary educational consultant for a company that designed educational software. Once they had a real, live English teacher at their disposal, they began to use me to write and edit other materials. Software documentation, marketing brochures, and presentations...I learned it all and loved it. The money was horrible, but the hours were flexible, I could work from home much of the time, and the experience was, as they say, priceless. I made it a point—and still do—to work with people who knew more than I did so I could learn from them.

So, when we moved next to Atlanta and then to Dayton, I could say in good conscience that I was a business writer. I had a client here and there, and for a while, I worked very part-time with a small advertising firm. Mostly, though, I volunteered. I was the room mother, the cookie mom, and, for one season, the soccer coach. When I volunteered for a cause, I picked agencies that I believed in, of course, but I also tried, as much as possible, to build my skills. I wanted to eventually evolve from a former teacher to a...I didn't know yet.

"I can stuff envelopes with the best of them, and I'm happy to do that. But why don't you let me write your _____." Fill in the blank. I stuffed plenty of envelopes, but I also wrote press releases and marketing plans, speeches, and letters begging for money. I did event planning, and I organized the work of other volunteers. They weren't paying me, so I could take as much time as I needed and get all the help necessary to do it right. By the time Daybreak, a runaway shelter in Dayton, wanted to hire me part-time to handle their public relations, I was getting excited about how my professional life, albeit a sporadic one, was turning out.

I admitted that I'd done all the pieces of a PR campaign but had never been in the driver's seat.

"That's okay," they said. "The money's an embarrassing joke."

"I'll do it for that amount of money," I said. "But I want a really great title."

As a result, in the next city and with the kids in high school, I hung out my shingle as a freelance public relations consultant. My resume was chock-full of great projects, and, fortunately, resumes do not require one to list how much—if anything—one got paid. With the top listing as "Public Relations Director," I was the peer of the other consultants I met, worked with, and learned from.

When the referrals began to come in, my consultant network friends asked me to please revise my rate card up, way up. "We can't refer people to you if you're going to charge so much less than we are," they told me. I didn't believe them when they said the clients would still come on board, but they were right. In addition, I hit the mother lode of mentors when I began to work with Andrea Eliscu, a national authority on medical marketing who needed help with the PR side of her business. She became a dear friend, and, although I taught her all I knew about PR in the first week or two, I'm still learning marketing from her today, eight years and 3,000 miles later.

The kids are now, quite simply, magnificent young women. My husband and I have no idea if they would have turned out better or worse had we made other choices, but they are happy with their lives, and so are we. Today I am a freelance, part-time PR and marketing consultant, specializing in medical marketing and work with non-profits. I pick and choose my clients and projects; my hobbies are cooking and working out to undo the damage of the first hobby; and I still handle all the "home business." I can drop everything when one of the girls—or my husband—needs me, and if I become a grandma, I will drop everything even more often. My husband and I are celebrating 29 years of marriage.

I still volunteer more than I work, but now it has a much fancier name: I work pro bono.

∼ A Balancing Act *by Christi Elflein* ∼

In the early 1990s, I was a college student with idealistic visions of going forward in life to make a difference. Who didn't, right? One particular class guest speaker made a lasting impression on me. She talked about being superwoman—world's best mom, super career woman, and fantastic wife. That's what I wanted to be—superwoman. I've worked toward that goal ever since. First I found the great career—urban planning. Then I found the perfect husband—Bill. We bought our first house, and now we have our first child, Jack. And am I now super-woman? No, I'm super TIRED!

Is there such a thing as a perfectly balanced life? Trying to be every-thing to everyone has only made me unhappy and unable to fully satis-fy all my obligations to the best of my ability. I've spent the last year and a half trying to figure out how to create the perfect balance in my life to be able to succeed in all three areas, as a mom, a career woman, and a wife. I have tried three experiments to find the right balance. First, I was a stay-home mom. Then, I went back to the boardroom part-time. Now, I've opened a home office.

My "balancing act" story really begins during my pregnancy. I was 30 years old and had been in the professional planning world for seven years, four years with my current company (we'll call the company "Planners R Us" for the purposes of this story). I was a star employee, a project manager, and well liked by both coworkers and clients.

I made the conscious decision before I left for maternity leave not to make any work status commitments until after Jack was born. After all, I had never been a mother before, and I didn't know what it was going to be like. Planners R Us likes to be known as being a family-friendly company and was very supportive of me during this time. I received a parking space close to our building; they threw me a great baby shower; and they left the door open for me to return whenever I was ready.

I stayed home for six months. This was my first experiment with finding the right balance. I loved that time that I had with Jack, but as many of you probably know, your job as mom isn't all just roses. Being a new mom has, by far, been the most challenging job I have ever had. And yes, it is a job. At the end of each day, I was burned out. I'd go to bed burned out, work through the night burned out, and wake up burned out. Each day began to run into the next, and before I knew it, I wasn't being the best mom (because I was TIRED), and I was a crabby wife (because I was TIRED). Additionally, my marriage started feeling the strain of my missing income. Experiment number one, a stay-home mom, was not the right balance for me. I commend all full-time stay-home moms for your selfless commitment!

Here begins experiment number two—going back to the boardroom. Going back to work, however, was not as easy as just showing up at the office. Three stars needed to align. First, Jack needed to start sleeping through the night, or else I would be a zombie at work, too. We're still working on perfecting this star, and I may have to wait for him to be a teenager before he wants to sleep more than Bill and I do. Second, I needed to come to an agreement with Planners R Us on how much time I would work every week. I was not quite ready to return full-time, and Planners R Us, being the family-friendly company that they are trying to be, kindly agreed to let me return at 20 hours per week. And the third and most important star, I had to find the right caregiver for Jack while I was at work.

Finding the right caregiver for Jack was much more challenging than I ever imagined. I put my name on the wait list for every reputable day-care center in the downtown area and started the search for a nanny, primarily by word of mouth. After lots of prayers, Marah and Jackson entered our lives. Marah was a friend of a friend of a friend who had a son, Jackson, the same age as Jack.

Enter the challenges. Challenge number one—money. Although $25 (my hourly wage) and $7 (Marah's hourly wage) sounds like a big difference, it wasn't. After paying employment taxes and the commuting costs, Marah cost us about $10 per hour. And after taxes were taken out of my salary, I made about $19 per hour. Then subtract the money it cost to have Marah from my salary, and I netted $9 per hour. What quality of bacon was I really bringing home?

Challenge number two—time. Plan, plan, plan all you want, but unpredictable sicknesses and last minute meetings throw those plans out the window. If the boys were sick or Marah couldn't change her schedule, I'd try to hire a different baby-sitter or rearrange client meetings. This juggling act wore on me.

Challenge number three—quality of work life. I had to make several concessions to return to work only part-time with Planners R Us. The largest concession I had to make was to step down as a project manager and play a more supportive role. At first, I thought this would be fine; and after a month of being back at Planners R Us, I thought things were going in the right direction. I had one foot in both worlds. I looked forward to coming home and seeing Jack, and I looked forward to going to work, having a change of scenery, and diving back into issues I was passionate about. Actually, I looked forward to going to work and having some time to sit in a quiet office by myself. I do believe it is easier to go to work all day than to stay home all day.

After a few months, doing special projects for people turned out to be more like answering to lots of people, and not being a project manager anymore became a worthless statement because no one wanted my one primary client, and by default they became mine again. So I was answering to both clients and partners. In a typical week, I was billing to eight to 12 projects. With only 20 hours per week of time committed, that meant I only had time to give lip service to any one of those projects. On top of this, the partners in charge of my department decided that because I was only part-time, I did not deserve to have an office with a window anymore. They needed to make room for the new hires, and I was moved to an internal office on an entirely separate floor from the rest of my group. My office was taken by a new male hire with several fewer years experience than I did. I was feeling demoted, demoralized, and completely unsupported.

It was time to have a conversation with my boss. I wanted to be reinstated as a project manager with a limited number of projects. She disagreed with this solution and gave me four options. One, come back to work full-time. Two, remain part-time and accept a supportive role. Three, change to a less demanding department. Or four, resign. The writing was on the wall that it was time for me to move on. So I chose to resign and go back to the drawing board to find that balance I so badly wanted. Looking closely at this arrangement, though, how could I improve on it?

First—money. Bringing home a higher quality of bacon to offset the cost of childcare would make working more worthwhile and would definitely be a plus. Second—time. I did not believe a total rework in the division of time was the answer. I did not want to take any more time away from Jack than I already had. Just a tweak of how the time was managed was needed. What I noticed was missing from the balance of time was "me" time. I had no time for myself, whether it was to exercise or have lunch with a friend. This definitely needed to be added into the daily routine. And to manage work time better, a more flexible childcare situation was necessary. Third-quality of work life. If I was going to be sacrificing time with Jack to work, then I wanted to be working on projects that I felt passionate about. And I wanted to work on fewer projects so that I could have the ability to do the quality of work that I want to do in the time I was committing to work.

My solution? For experiment number three, I made two significant changes. First, Jack was accepted into a good daycare where he is enrolled full-time; however, I only take him part-time. This situation gives me the flexibility to take him whenever I want during the day, allowing my schedule to remain flexible and allowing me to add an additional hour into my day for "me" time. Second, I have started my own consulting firm. I am able to schedule my own hours, set my hourly rate at my true value, and choose the projects that I want to work on.

I am in the early stages of trying out balance experiment number three; therefore, I cannot give you an accurate assessment of the situation. However, they say the third time is the charm, and I feel that I am on the right track. There are new challenges. It is difficult to drop Jack off at daycare (we both generally shed a few tears), but when I pick him up, he's having a ball, and I can tell he is enjoying the interaction with other children his age. I am enjoying the flexibility, and I truly enjoy the type of work that I am doing.

What I have realized over the past year and a half is that going back to work is not just about bringing home the bacon—it's about me, and it's about my family. It's about creating meaning in my life. It's about finding a balance in my life and being a happy person so that I can be the best mother and wife that I can be. So I guess my quest for a perfect balance has turned into an acceptance of lead character of the endless juggling act in this circus of life.

∼ The Best of Both Worlds *by Lisa Starr, M.Ed.* ∼

I have been home now for two years. It almost seems like yesterday when I would make the trek to my job, day in and day out. I sit back in the morning and listen to the traffic report and don't have to worry if I should leave a little bit earlier because when there is an accident on I-95 North, it seems like it takes forever just to get to work.

No longer am I rushing in the morning to beat the clock to get to the boardroom. Instead, I am facing my three handsome sons, to get them up and ready for the classroom. I have a three-year-old, Justin, who is my escort all day. It almost seemed as if I was that mothering figure at the job, but he is much different from managing coworkers all day.

Each day, you really don't know what to expect. I am a firm believer in making sure your children have a set schedule. They go to bed, wake up, eat breakfast, and prepare for the day on a set schedule. I would not have it any other way. Their schedule gives them and me a sense of direction daily. My kids are the highlight of every day. I make sure I prepare a hot breakfast every day. They look forward to spending some time at the breakfast table talking about life. It feels good to be a part of their lives on a daily basis. When they come home, it's homework before playtime.

When I traveled, it would break my heart to call from an exclusive hotel in Puerto Rico, The Ritz-Carlton, to speak to my kids, and they would always say, "When are you coming home to spend time with us?" I would cry and never get any sleep when I was away.

It really hit me hard when Reggie was talking one evening at the dinner table and he said, "You don't spend much time with us in the evening anymore." I knew I had to make some changes. I would often question myself at this time of my journey. "How much longer will it be before I take the dive into being a full-time stay-at-home mom?"

So, I went back to graduate school, hoping to open my very own home business so that I could spend more time with my children. Well, my reality has come true. My kids tell me 24/7, you are the best mom in the whole wide world! It warms my heart to know I make a difference in the world of my children. Summers used to be a hustle to day camp to drop them off; instead, we are spending time reading together, going to local children's events, and just sitting poolside. My oldest son, Reggie, said to me as we were sitting outside on the hammock looking up into the sky, "This is the life! I love when you spend time with me. You're the best!"

I finished my master's degree in education, and I am currently teaching edible art classes to children in the evening. Since taking control of how I decide to spend my time, I feel a stronger connection with my sons. I am the playgroup/support group coordinator of the Mocha Moms, Woodbridge Chapter in Virginia. We get together to discuss pertinent topics, go on trips, and get together for potlucks. I have time to go to the gym to work out. My kids love to go to the gym with me; they are constantly reminding me, "Mom, are we going to the kids' zone?" They are great motivators to inspire me to get out of the house to go work out. I am a strong believer in taking care of self. If you don't feel good, your family won't feel good, either.

My parents are both deceased within the past two years. They were both schoolteachers who spent the entire summer home with my three sisters and me. I had two wonderful role models who spent endless time with me. I will say it was these memories that I will cherish forever!

I often ask myself, "What memories will my children remember about me?" And, now I have my answer. My sons realize how lucky and blessed they really are since I am at home. They appreciate all of my time, and I would not have it any other way. I will never go back to the nine-to-five bustle! I am able to make my own schedule, spend time to raise my sons, and feel a stronger connection with my sons.

Education has always been really important in my family. My oldest son the other day said, "When I go to college for the first time..." I immediately had tears in my eyes! Then my middle son, Brandon, said, "I'm going to college, too." I believe teaching kids at a young age is important. I have always stressed the importance of school and what journey is necessary for survival.

I heard a quote that has changed my life: "You are pregnant with potential; give birth to your dreams!" My dream of being a full-time mother with an at-home business has come true.

I've been married for ten years to my husband, Reggie Starr. He has always inspired me to follow my dreams. His favorite saying is "Just Do It!" As a wife and a mother, having a family has always been important to me. I feel a stronger sense of connection with my kids than ever before. I know I will cherish these memories for a lifetime. Being a mother, you will definitely learn time-management skills, how to balance life, and how to enjoy the many challenges of being an unforgettable MOM!

∿ Teetering on the Balance Beam of Life as a New Mom *by Deidre Groehnert* ∿

In the 13th year of my successful career in Corporate America, I found myself pregnant. Not coming as a surprise in the conventional sense of: "Oops, how did that happen?", it was a surprise because I had been sure that this last fertility treatment was going to fail like all the rest, and I had resigned myself to adopting a child. This attempt came at the end of four years of fertility treatments that had battered my optimism, tested my marriage, and caused hormonally-induced chaos with my mental state. Maybe because I had finally given up and let go a bit, the ultimate reward was now a tangible possibility!

To work or not to work, is that the question?

So, during 40 weeks of excitement, smiling through the nausea, laughing through the back pain, I deliberated about my future life as a mommy. Since a girl of five years old, I had a clear picture of myself becoming a mommy, but it was always a mommy AND an artist or a mommy AND a teacher. The AND would fluctuate from year to year, but the mommy part always remained. So, now that my dream was coming to fruition, I couldn't help but wonder...how will I balance motherhood with womanhood; career with caregiving; creative outlets with creating life? In the same way that Carrie Bradshaw tried to solve the mystery of men, I tried to unravel the mystery of my new role in life. I would have to settle on the title following the AND. I wanted my mother role to be top priority but had no desire for my mind to atrophy or our bills to go unpaid. I did some research and soul-searching.

I had many discussions in my head, as well as with other women, about the balance and sacrifices that were to come. The financial uncertainty if I were to derail my career for a while seemed daunting, as did the emotional uncertainty of leaving my newborn under someone else's care if I did not. I looked to others for an answer that was unwittingly hiding within me. And as I discussed work/life balance with mothers of young children, I learned that being a part of a generation with more options has created an epidemic of uncertainty, guilt, and insecurity.

This is a most unfortunate consequence to gaining our freedoms. The insecurity chimes through when women discuss the topic. Many conversations I had with stay-at-home moms (SAHMs) rapidly turned into a discussion of how working moms don't care enough; and, all too often, when I spoke to working mothers, they seemed to seek solace in discussing how "SAHMs" don't do enough. My gut told me to stay at home and work from home, and keep out of the battle all together! It was just going to be tough swinging the bills, so I couldn't rule out full-time work. As my belly swelled and everything was only theoretical, I just enjoyed gliding through pregnancy without making a firm decision.

And along came Tommy...ready or not, on October 19, an 11-pound, two-ounce redheaded blue-eyed angel was handed to me, and I have been madly in love with this "little" creature ever since! Once my son Tommy came into my life, everything changed. Motherhood would prove to be a sweeter tonic than I was prepared for, on the one hand, but also generated some of the most trying and upsetting moments of my life. After a four-hour crying jag, you really dig deep for patience; and when your toddler takes a nasty fall, you wish it was you, and you feel their pain deeply. No one could have properly prepared me for this roller coaster of emotions that had a thread of joy woven through both the good and bad moments. I had been enrobed in a new kind of warm love and accepted a more important job than I had ever had before. The product of this new job would hopefully be a well-adjusted, healthy, and loving adult.

However, as lovely and intense as motherhood was, it did not eradicate the need to pay bills or the desire to use my higher mind occasionally! Once the fog of those first three sleepless months lifted, the realities had to be dealt with.

Fortunately, at about this time, I was spared one very difficult choice. As I continued to waver on the topic of returning to work-the universe sent me a clear message in the form of a phone call. The corporation I worked for was doing massive layoffs, and I was that day's casualty. This was a blessing for me, although the details of the situation took away some of the pleasure, and no one likes to lose a job...this situation brought much more upside than down. I could now build my career at home with a clean slate and no immediate financial worries (the severance pay and unemployment kept us going, and both had been earned, I assure you).

Turning my passion into profit, I found building a new career from scratch both scary financially and also exciting. I kept an open mind with only one caveat-I would not sell anything. Not baskets, not makeup, not bathroom brushes, or overpriced cutlery; not homes, not mortgages, not the dream of a better day. Not my soul, not a toothpick...I would not sell. Anything. Everywhere I turned, there were work-at-home job opportunities...to sell. I thwarted them, resenting the fact that so many women with assorted talents were being ignored or forced to sell if they wanted flexibility or to work from home. I would beat the odds and find a lucrative career working from home that did not involve selling.

I started by analyzing the career I had before children, to identify the tasks that most inspired me. I wanted to find my passion, believing that the money would come later if only I was passionate about the work. I knew when I had been called upon to write training curricula, Web sites, or newsletters, I had always enjoyed the creativity writing brought. Writing was the passion I would pursue. I loved to help people see a new perspective or learn something new through my words. With my years of experience, it should be easy to build a business as a writer at home, right?

So, while my baby napped, I wrote. When he went to sleep for the night, I wrote. When Daddy bathed him, I wrote. First, creating children's tales, then taking on small corporate writing jobs (which dried up quickly), then becoming the writer and editor of a regional parenting Web site. Writing for the parent Web site took up all my free time and brought in little money but led to becoming a contributor of parenting articles to that same company's national Web site. This helped me build confidence and a collection of published works to use as samples.

This newfound confidence led to submitting articles to national magazines. I sent articles to many magazines and sent my children's tales to every publisher and agent I could find and continued to struggle with tiny paychecks from the Internet writing. I gave copies of my children's stories to published authors and illustrators at book signings, and still no luck. My career as a writer was only taking baby steps. What kept me going were some new friends who were women building their own businesses and balancing the business with their devotion to their kids. Fellow mothers (when not being catty) can be the most wonderful and supportive friends! These "in-betweeners," working flexible hours like me, would teach me to have faith that the bills would get paid and to keep trying. Somehow they always did, miraculously, get paid. Every time I was about to give up, some type of check would come in the mail, or a surprise would arrive. One time, just before Christmas, I used some of my last few cash dollars to go into a church raffle and won the top prize—a basket filled with Christmas items. This had to be a sign. I was a Christmas fanatic! So onward I trudged.

Over a year passed, savings dwindled, stocks were sold to cover bills, old junk was sold in a garage sale, belts were tightened, and grandparents were generous. It really continued to bother me that a disappointing number of companies were willing to employ SAHMs, no matter how experienced or hardworking. Yet, the answer to my frustration did not seem to come in toiling away as a poor writer. Being a "starving artist" seemed a lot less romantic as a 30-something mom with a mortgage than it did as a freewheeling 20-something! With a family, I didn't have the luxury of waiting around for submitted articles to be published or children's tales to hit the shelves of a bookstore; I had to make a change. Although we had somehow made it this far, I started getting desperate.

Desperate is a place filled with opportunity. My greatest inspiration comes during desperation. With nothing to lose, I thought: "What the hell, I might as well sell!" I chose to give up my preconception that selling was the evil vortex that sucked in SAHMs yearning for extra income. I dropped the notion that I would be a terrible salesperson and gave it a go. I still believed that there should be many more options available to SAHMs, but at one point, you need to take a break from trying to change the world and work within its current boundaries. I had developed a strong gut feeling that for me the right thing was to be available for my young child as often as I could. I also needed to be home while trying for another baby (before my fertility-challenged biological clock completely blew up!). I wanted my 20-month-old son in a short preschool program, mornings some days and with me all day other days, so that we could both have balance, and he could gain socialization skills.

I took a position selling advertising space on the Web site I helped create, a product I really believed in. I swam with the tide in my life, instead of fighting it—selling was the next logical step at that small but growing mother-founded company. Selling would have greater potential earnings, alleviating much of my financial worry and stress. During my first month of sales, a strange thing happened. I started to enjoy the challenge of creating the perfect proposal. Also, I forged strong connections with clients because of my honest and helpful "non-sales approach" to sales. Month one and I almost tripled my sales goal. I was on my way and finally comfortable that I could stay home for a while longer and keep up with the bills.

This is now my answer, my answer for right now. I will sacrifice the momentum I had in business and the big paychecks to be able to spend more time teaching Tommy that he is loved, that life is filled with adventures, and how important it is to love himself and others. If those lessons stay with him through his life, that will be my biggest payoff.

Ask me next month how I am finding balance in my life, and I may have a different recipe for success. The only thing I know for sure is that nothing is for sure. I am blessed that I let go of my certainty and took a forbidden path that led to success. I am also grateful for every moment I get to spend with my lovely son. His laughter fills my heart, and with each passing day, he finds new ways to make me laugh and gives me more reasons to dance. What I have learned in the last two years is to keep an open mind, trust my gut, don't judge other moms, don't worry too far into the future, and to receive each day with Tommy as the gift that it is. And, ladies, until the day comes when, through our collective entrepreneurial spirits, there emerges a business environment where working at home becomes widespread across careers, I say: What the hell-sell!

∼ Bye-Bye Boardroom, Hello Life! ∼
by Donna Maria Coles Johnson

It was 1998, and I was living what many would consider to be a wonderful lifestyle, and it was. I was working as an attorney at a Fortune 500 corporation in Washington, DC, and my life was filled with every material thing a person could desire. I earned a six-figure salary including bonuses, health benefits, stock options, and other perks. I enjoyed several weeks of paid vacation each year, drove a luxury car, lived in an upscale neighborhood, and ate out as often as I liked, wherever I liked. I was a rising star in the corporate world, with a job most people my age would have killed to have. I had done what my parents taught me to do: Go to school and get a good job. I was hard at work pursuing prosperity, security, and prestige, and living a lifestyle that many people could only dream of. I was in Professional Utopia, except for one thing.

I was miserable.

Every morning, along with several of my coworkers, I arrived at work after an hour-long commute (more if there was an accident or inclement weather) to take my seat in an office with windows facing across an alley where I could wave to another rising star and wonder whether she was as tortured as I was. After a day answering hundreds of e-mail messages, participating in conference calls, meeting with directors and vice presidents, inhaling lunch at my desk, and generally trying to prove myself worthy of the next bonus, pay raise, or promotion, it was seven or eight in the evening, and there was still more work to be done.

Everything around me was a blur. One of the things that bothered me the most was seeing women struggle to raise their children and be wives to their husbands while pursuing the pot of gold at the end of the corporate rainbow. They frequently dragged themselves into the office, wiping tears from their eyes because they had left their little ones in daycare an hour's drive away. If there was an infant at home, they were often exhausted long before arriving at the office. It was clear to me that even a healthy bank account could not make up for what I would miss if I were ever in their shoes.

So, one summer day, I gave two weeks notice to a very stunned vice president and set off to create a life I could enjoy from the inside out. Now, eight years later, I am fulfilling my highest callings for this time in my life. I am a wife and mother of two beautiful children. I participate in field trips and take weekday trips to the zoo, pumpkin patches, and strawberry farms whenever I want to. I enjoy picnic lunches during the week, and I do my grocery shopping when no one else is in the store.

Today, instead of working in someone else's boardroom, I work in my own—a very small home office right next to my children's playroom. There are toy blocks under the desk, Magic Marker doodles on the floor, stuffed animals on the bookshelf, and sticky fingerprints on the windows. There are probably multigrain cereal rounds in the fax machine! I would never say it's easy. At times, it's completely chaotic, juggling dirty dishes, unfolded clothes, and a customer issue all at the same time. But, despite the challenges, it's MY chaos. I created it, and I manage it, and I wouldn't have it any other way.

I call myself and women like me "Lifestyle CEOs." I trademarked that term to describe us as women who own and manage a business, not solely for financial gain but also to enjoy the personal rewards of entrepreneurship, independence, flexibility, and fun. We are breaking all the rules, climbing our own corporate ladders, and enjoying our personal lives and careers on our own terms.

The best part about my story is that any determined woman can become a Lifestyle CEO in her own right. With a little planning and ingenuity, creativity and help, we can slough off the old corporate chains like yesterday's dry skin and make lives that suit us, instead of trying to fit our lifestyles into someone else's idea of what a professional woman and mother can and should be.

CHAPTER 8

SO, THIS IS ME!

~ **Becoming Mommy** *by Ann-Marie Dombrowski* ~

Growing up, I never dreamed of becoming a stay-at-home mom. I knew I wanted children but never thought I would leave my career to have them. So, making the transition from being a career-oriented woman to being a stay-at-home mom with a three-month-old was very difficult. For me, what made the transition even harder was moving away from the city I grew up in for a house in the hills, something my husband and I believed would be best for our child. Leaving my family and friends, my support group, was especially tough on me. Without a job to go to everyday, I felt like I left my entire life behind for the benefit of my baby.

I have spent so many guilty days and nights fighting my every being, my every urge to want to go back to work. There were days when I would look at my little princess, scoop her into my arms, and cry my eyes out. I was racked with guilt over wanting to leave my precious angel to return to work. In those moments, I would think, "How could dealing with the corporate world ever compare to what I have right now?" My daughter is growing so quickly everyday, and everyday she manages to amaze me. I wondered, "Am I just not maternal enough to stay home with my baby?"

I was so unprepared for motherhood. I didn't know any nursery rhymes or children's songs, so when she would cry, I would softly sing her the ABCs. I kept reminding myself that as long as I was there to love her, feed her, and keep her safe, it should be enough for me. I didn't need to work. But then, someone would ask what I did for a living, and I would say I was "just a stay-at-home mom." I thought people looked down on me as if I wasn't good enough. As if I was not important enough because

I had no career to name or to speak of. In those moments, why was I not, instead, filled with pride and joy over having a little girl who filled my heart and my life with love? Her beautiful laugh and all the wonderful things about her sometimes made me feel so overwhelmed with love, like a mother cub protecting her young. Certainly, staying home should have felt like the right thing to do, so why did I feel so horrible at times for wanting a break? I longed to get away.

Finally, I spoke to a friend (a still working friend) who told me I should hold my head up high. She said that most women in the corporate world with children would die to stay home with them. I am lucky enough to be able to witness every "first" in my daughter's life. Most working parents don't have the good fortune to be able to experience even half of their child's firsts.

I spent so much time and guilt thinking I wanted to go back to work, all the while not completely enjoying every moment spent with my daughter, because I thought I was missing out on something "out there." I was wrong. I am not missing anything. I am witness to the greatest miracle of all!

Since that conversation with my working friend, I have made it a point to enjoy every moment with my little girl. No more fussing or whining on my part. Our little one does the only whining in our house. I don't fuss over the paint splatter on the walls or curtains. We'll clean up once we are done having fun. I've even gone so far as to show her how to wipe her mouth with her sleeve, because it's kind of cute; and after all, we only live once. Who cares, they're just clothes, and that's what washing machines are for.

My daughter has taught me to be more relaxed. Instead of rushing to get our "to do list" done, we stroll down the street (at her pace) enjoying our outings. It's funny because my husband is the one who's always in a rush, which makes any shopping trip with him a disaster. He is trying to learn that even if you do it slowly, it will still get done. And my sister told me needing a break is normal. My husband and I call our breaks "mental health days." So every once in a while, I leave my daughter at home with my husband and go out and do something for myself—without the guilt.

I am complete! My daughter and I are perfect together! No one can be goofier than we are. We laugh and play all day. It's amazing what little ones can accomplish when they've got their mom home with them.

My daughter has learned her ABCs and counts from one to 20 in English and from one to ten in Spanish; she has also learned the colors in a box of crayons and lots of different shapes, all before the age of two and a half. She's learned these things because I'm home to teach her. Learning is fun in our home and so is cleaning up.

She's thriving physically, mentally, and emotionally, not because I work 16-plus hours a day but because those 16-plus hours are spent with her. My job may not be listed on any application, but it's fulfilling. This job may not come with vacation days or even days off, but it's full with lots of laughter. This job may not come with a paycheck, but the reward is there...in every smile, in every step, every picture on the refrigerator, and every accomplishment.

We do have our bad days, but no matter; the good days outweigh the bad a million times over.

I am a stay-at-home mom!

∼ **Bra Burners** *by Gina DiPaolo* ∼

I am a woman. I am proud and blessed to be one. I embrace all that I am and my potential to be more. I realize the sacrifices women before me have made so that I enjoy a life filled with choices. So many choices, in fact, that many times in my life, I've been fooled into thinking I can do it all with smart organizing. Or sometimes I am paralyzed with indecision because of the number of choices I have. I am fearful of making a choice that will leave me empty or unfulfilled. This is a crime in my generation.

Oftentimes I wonder who is better off—my mother or me? My mother graduated from college in 1964, and at that time, her career choices were nurse, teacher, secretary, or airline stewardess. When I graduated from college in 1989, I had roughly 200 options. She married immediately after college and started a family within three years, following closely the social custom of the day. I ventured to a new city with my degree, spread my wings, and lived on my own. I did marry, but not before really questioning myself: Do I really need to get married? Or can I accomplish what I need to without the "piece of paper." I mean, I was raised to support myself and stand on my own.

Next came the question of children. Since I hadn't said "no way" before our marriage, I felt compelled to consider the option. But how would I juggle motherhood and career? Could I leave my child with a nanny? I am a control freak; a nanny seemed like an iffy option. How would I handle my full schedule of volunteering? How could I combine all these and still appear effortlessly beautiful and the life of the party? According to the rules laid out by my generation, I could and would handle everything because many women were also doing it. And while this seemed logical, my uneasiness existed on many levels.

Honestly, sometimes I curse the women who burned their bras—the women who fought for and brought attention to the inequality of men and women during that time. The pendulum of life had swung too far for them. And their revolution started the pendulum on its trip the other way—the way toward higher awareness, empowerment, and choice. Somewhere, as it started to pick up speed, I got swept up on the pendulum. And I, like many other women of my generation, got caught in the aftermath. We weren't part of the revolution or the creation of the new world order, but now we must play the game according to rules we didn't create. And while the game seems fun, the longer you play, the more you realize you have no more freedom, really, than your mom did. You are just trapped in a different set of circumstances and judged by a different, although just as confining, set of rules—rules that tell you, you can effectively be a career woman and a wife and mother. Rules that say you can conceive and give birth whenever you choose. You can climb the corporate ladder as high as you want. You can be a man.

I wonder, in all that I've gained, have I lost my sense of power over my life? If I don't do it all, am I letting the women around me down? Am I breaking the code? What scares me about the bra burners is that they say women can be men. Women don't need men. In all their rationalizing, did they realize they might be letting go of the core of what woman is? In striving to be more like men, rejecting the emotional, nurturing paths, have they effectively left a generation of women not understanding what it means to be a woman? Squelching the innate power and beauty that exists in each feminine soul? Not honoring the beauty of compassion, the power of serving, the heartbeat of a family?

I say no. It does seem that way to me sometimes as I grapple with all my choices, but I still see my generation as the pendulum riders who have seen the apex of the swing and now have the opportunity to forge a path to what my mother calls the happy medium. That place in the arc of the swing where things settle nicely. The extremes have been experienced and refined and softened. I do think my generation has experienced the extreme. And the repercussions of that will be reflected in the children we raise and women we grow to be. We've had to try to make sense of all the choices. And it begs the questions: Just because we can, should we? Or how about just because we can, do we want to? My generation hasn't had the choice. The idea sold to me was that "Women before you have fought for this. Enjoy your power and freedom."

Nobody asked if we really wanted to. It was more like, what's wrong with you if you don't want it all? Just because we can have a high-powered career, be married, and raise children all at once, do we want to? Just because medically it is possible to give birth in your mid 40s, do we want to? I have learned that many of these opportunities and choices come with lots of fine print. And the truth is: Choices have costs and parameters.

So, that brings me to my original question. Am I better off than my mother? Yes. Thank you, bra burners. It's been an interesting ride. But now having come to peace and understanding about history and learning to utilize my choices, my job as a woman is far from over. I have an obligation to my peers, my predecessors, and myself to continue along the arc and help drive the birth of a new generation of women. It is my hope that my daughter will experience true freedom of choice. I will teach her to make use of all the options available to her while not forgetting the beauty and fragility that is woman. I will tell my daughter she can do anything she wants, but she can't do it all and do it well. The key to true empowerment is living a life of purpose.

∼ First Day of School *by Carlyle Spina* ∼

As I lay in the hospital bed recovering from the birth of my newborn twins, I willed myself to look ahead for some glimmer of hope. Instead of beaming with joy, I literally cringed as I peered over the bassinet where my tiny babies were sleeping, overwhelmed by the thought of raising and nurturing these two unbelievably small and very needy creatures. At that dark moment, the hope that propelled me forward was the thought that one day I would drop them off for their first day of school.

Today is that day. The day of my liberation, my semi-release from the 24/7 day-to-day clutches of being a mom, and the day I have been waiting a lifetime for, or at least the last six years. Today my children embark on their academic journey...kindergarten.

My heart breaks a little bit as they enter the front door in their cute little uniforms, having no clue what lies before them.

"Mama?" My daughter Kit looks back for support and begs the burning question, "You won't forget to pick us up?" As if I've been convicted of this type of crime before.

"Of course not, I'll be right here and so excited to hear about your first day!" My son Van flashes a dorky grin and proceeds through the door resolutely, prepared to take on kindergarten as skillfully as pre-k.

For the first time ever, they'll be choosing and cultivating their own little friendships. This approach is in sharp contrast to the previous method whereby play dates were arranged based on whether I thought I could hang with the mom for a period of time. Designing but necessary, and even if the kids don't initially dig each other, they do eventually. But that may not fly anymore.

I feel a tug, a sense of sadness and fear mixed with absolute jubilation. They've been my constant companions for the last few years, and in that time I've become quite comfortable in my new role as mama, camp counselor, and enforcer, among many others. Parenthood is a responsibility I took on very deliberately, yet I assumed the role of motherhood reluctantly. At first I didn't seem to fit the mold. Giving up my career, staying home with my kids, planning meals, shopping at Target, heading to the zoo or park or museum with kids in tow were not what I had envisioned for myself when my husband and I made the decision to start a family. I somehow thought kids would simply embellish my already full and happy life. Not completely overtake it and reshape it into something barely resembling what it was before. But that's what motherhood did for me. And I've discovered I do fit the mold. Motherhood fits me like a glove.

And with the same naiveté, I release my children into academia. Now I am certain to fill my days with some feverish importance? I feel a need to reclaim some part of myself, start where I left off but knowing that's impossible, having submerged myself into the most important job of all. On this day, I look ahead to when they really won't need me anymore. The first day of high school? Perhaps.

Now what? I head to Starbucks.

◇ An Attitude Worth Catching ◇
by Lynne Ticknor, M.A.

When I was the training and development manager for a large financial services company, I often asked the managers who attended my leadership courses, "Attitudes are contagious—is yours worth catching?" There is nothing new in the question. It's been asked for years. I can't even track down the individual who first coined the phrase. But, I know it's a powerful question because it generated a lot of discussion in the corporate world, and many people tell me that they still remember when I asked them that question over a decade ago.

Now I'm a stay-at-home mom, and I ask myself, "Is my attitude worth catching?" Sometimes it's a scary thought.

As the leader of my family, the way I think, feel, and act affects not only my own life but also the lives of everyone around me. A positive attitude gives energy—to me and to those who spend time with me. A negative attitude drains it.

It's not surprising that many of us SAHMs suffer from negativity. In his book, *What a Great Idea!* Charles Thompson reveals that parents utter 18 negative statements to children for every one positive statement, usually to an inquisitive preschooler who is just trying to understand how things work. If my son asks, "Mommy, what makes the sky blue?" and I reply with an impatient, "I don't know, does it really matter?" I am contributing to the 432 negative statements parents make every day!

I've come to realize that attitude is nothing more than a mind-set—it's the way I look at life and the things that happen around me. And, I have the power to change it. As I go through my day, I often ask myself if I am seeing the glass as half empty or half full. By training myself to always see the glass as half full—by identifying the good parts of each situation rather than focusing on the negative—I often make great strides in improving my attitude.

I had a positive attitude when I was going to the office every morning—to a job I loved, with people I respected and admired—but now that I am at home with three (soon to be four) demanding children, that powerful, pithy phrase, "Is Your Attitude Worth Caching?" haunts me. Several times throughout the day, I'll take note of my attitude and how negative it is. The other day when my husband called to say he was going to be late getting home from work, I found myself having all sorts of negative thoughts (he's always late coming home from work; now the pot roast is going to be dried out; how am I going to keep the kids entertained for another 45 minutes, etc.). Instead, I could have filled my head with "glass half full" thinking, which would have gone something like this: He's only late when he's working on a big project; now the potatoes will have time to cool before serving them; I can use this extra time to read to the kids (or do something else we all enjoy).

It's easy for me to get caught up in the stress of being home with young children every day, and that's usually when my attitude first begins to suffer. I often feel like I am on one of those old-fashioned playground merry-go-round spinning things that several kids can get on at a time, and other kids spin them round and round. I want to get off, but all the kids around me are laughing and screaming, spinning me faster and faster. I can't jump off because I'll crash and burn, and no one is listening to my pleas of discomfort. Once the ride has ended, I am dizzy and exhausted. (I haven't seen these on playgrounds for years—I'm sure they've been banned as too dangerous, just as bad attitudes need to be banned!)

On days like that, I can get short-tempered and, well...downright crabby. My attitude suffers, and I start having negative thoughts. Then, it's inevitable, once my attitude heads for the toilet, so too do my children's. I can see it in their behavior. When my attitude is negative (read: "I'm tired and I don't feel like playing Thomas the Tank Engine trains anymore!"), my kids are whiny and disagreeable. If, on the other hand, I stay positive throughout the day (read: "I enjoy seeing you have so much fun when we play Thomas the Tank Engine"), I get cooperation and agreeable behavior.

It sure was easier to maintain a positive attitude when I worked in corporate America, but it's more important that I have one during my time at home with the kids. With a positive attitude, I'm teaching my children an important lesson. And, my positive attitude, affirming statements, and upbeat behavior rub off on them. When they "catch" my positive attitude, I know I'm headed toward a more enjoyable day of parenting!

∼ I Get It Now *by Elizabeth La Pietra DeWoody* ∼

Imagine it all being taken away...the good with the bad. What if you had to sit on the sidelines and watch your family in motion? No more being a mother. Just hang out and take care of yourself for about four months. Now, four months ago, if someone had told me I could take care of just myself, I would have been ecstatic.

I remember the good old days. I was on the fast track at Procter & Gamble, one out of 500 to receive an offer from P&G. I thought this was it. Great money, company car, travel, recognition, promotions, cool, innovative, exciting people. Awesome! And it was ALL about me. I was the youngest on my sales team and promoted to management as the youngest on the management team. That was the way I liked it—FAST and first to accomplish everything. It was an adrenaline rush. Getting married and having babies was the last thing on my mind, as my goal was to make well into six figures before I turned 30. (Gosh, I sound like such a bitch now!!)

Then, I made the switch to a medical sales job with Johnson & Johnson, another top-notch Fortune 500. My main concern was where my name fell in the sales ranking report and what I was going to wear to the next sales meeting. I won trips to places like Hawaii and Paris. It was amazing. My husband and I were dual income world travelers, and we had a blast! It drives me crazy when my new mom friends wonder what they did with their time before kids. I remember! And it was great!!

Then, my first baby came along. Oh my...what a shocker. I will never forget leaving my sales team a message from the hospital with the update, ensuring everyone that I would be back soon. I remember calling my manager and setting a date of exactly three months for my return. I could not wait to get back to work. I was HUGE. My boobs were HUGE and leaking, and I hadn't slept in weeks!!

"What about ME?" I exclaimed to my mom.

"What about you??? It is not about you. It is about your baby now! You need to get over thinking about yourself all the time," she replied.

I was furious! She did not get it. She did not have a college degree, a master's degree, and ten years invested in a burgeoning career. How could she understand?

So, I hired a full-time nanny and went back to work. I had it all mapped out just like everything else in my life. Thankfully, my nanny was terrific, and she spoke English and Spanish. Kent was speaking Spanish and English before he turned two! I thought that was so important. (Typical first-time mom.) I worked out of my house, had flexibility at work, and basically had it all, or so I thought! Until I started falling more and more in love with this little person, my son Kent. I started to care less about what I was going to wear to the national sales meeting and more about how I could get out of going. Getting on a plane and spending the night in a hotel room for three nights was the last thing I wanted to do. I could not bear leaving my beautiful baby with someone else for days at a time.

In order for me to continue growing and moving forward with my career, travel and relocation were a must. However, I found I was just no longer fulfilled working in the big corporate machine. It all seemed so shallow to me now. Somehow, somewhere in the middle of it all, IT had started to be not just about me. Wow! Could my mother have been right?? After my second baby, my husband and I decided to make some changes. I was determined to find a career that was fulfilling while combining my desire to be at home with my family. I will never forget what one of my very dear friends said to me during this transition in my life. She said, "Liz, you will always be able to go back to work. But, your children will never be babies again." A profoundly true statement from a friend who had found the joy in motherhood very early on in her life. Little did I know that I would soon be so grateful for her advice.

I decided I would leave the fast-track life and take some time away from it all to be with my boys, Kent, then two, and Casey, a newborn, and my WONDERFUL husband Don. I would take some time to figure out what I could do next. I loved taking Kent to school and hanging out with Casey. But, I felt my mind turning to mush. I missed the constant reward and recognition I had received at work. I missed MY time, when "IT" was about me. I missed my dynamic, interesting friends at work. I missed having interesting things to talk to my husband about. Play groups and some of the mom friends I met just were not getting it done for me. I needed to create something to rejuvenate my soul and my mind.

I continued to struggle with only being "a mom." I still wanted to have another dimension in my life. It seemed like such a waste to have invested so much time and energy into an education and career and then surrender to changing diapers, potty training, and breaking up fights. A book! I would write a book about how hard it was to make the transition and how different our generation of motherhood is from our mothers. Then I could have one more baby, a cool, fulfilling job, and have it all again!

I still did not get it!

The day I was planning to meet my girlfriend for lunch to discuss my book proposal is the same day I received the phone call that changed my life and perspective about motherhood, marriage, and work forever. "We see a little malignancy" brought me to my knees. A breast biopsy confirmed I HAD BREAST CANCER! I had no idea you could get breast cancer at 37 years old! And I certainly never planned on being the FIRST one to get breast cancer! Was I going to die? All I could think about was what about my children and my husband!! IT was truly not about me anymore.

The last year has been a journey that has changed my perspective and outlook on motherhood and life forever.

I think I get IT now.

Imagine checking out for four months. Putting your life on hold and setting up systems for other people to care for your children. No matter how much planning and preparation I did, nothing could prepare me for the feelings of helplessness, fear, isolation, and the overwhelming desire just to be able to NOT have to rely on a system of planning. I just wanted to be with my children. First came the mastectomy. I left surgery with these enormous, hard implants called expanders, and drains inserted in each side of my chest. My amazing husband emptied my drains and changed my bandages for two weeks. I was "pumped up" every ten days in order to stretch the skin in preparation for the implants. It hurt so bad that I could not even hug, much less hold, my Casey boy. Before surgery, every morning, Casey would climb up in bed with me and snuggle while he sucked his thumb and lay on my chest. Now he was going to my husband's side of the bed and climbing up with him to snuggle because he couldn't get comfortable on Mommy's boobs anymore. I could no longer pick him up and let him put his head on my shoulder. These are some of the simple pleasures I was not prepared to mourn the loss of.

Then came the chemo. I was not sure what to expect. My girlfriend, who was diagnosed with breast cancer merely weeks before me and was also going through the same chemo regime I was about to embark on, told me to move my mother down for three months because the unexpected was all I could expect. What? No planning, no control, and my mom helping my husband take care of my kids? Now, I was forced to surrender motherhood entirely!

I spent six weeks in my bedroom at 6:30 a.m. listening to my husband make breakfast, assemble lunches, get two boys dressed for school, himself dressed for work, and everyone out the door by 7:30. It drove me crazy! I had no control. Don was truly amazing! However, it broke my heart hearing him rally the troops on his own every morning: "Eat, get dressed, and brush your teeth." Then, he would take them both to school, and I would not see them until around 4:00 in the afternoon. I had no idea what they wore to school, what they ate for breakfast, and was even deprived of the sweet sight of my baby boys. The simple things were what I discovered I missed the most. I would do anything to actually have the energy to get up, cook breakfast, make lunches, and take them to school. Those simple "mindless" things that I once considered insignificant were now all that I was yearning to do.

Kent, my five-year-old, has always had a hair fetish. He did not suck his thumb and rub his blanket like my baby. He liked to rub my hair. It drove me nuts! Before he went to bed, he wanted to rub my hair. When he would get really tired, he liked to sit on my lap and rub my hair. I don't know, it was just his thing. At about two weeks into chemo, my hair started thinning. Kent came home from school, ran to the couch, and jumped up on me to give me a hug. Of course, he proceeded to rub my hair.

"Mommy, your hair is falling out," he announced, with a clump of my hair in his hand. I started crying and laughing at the same time. Shortly thereafter, I shaved my head and am still bald. I would give anything to lie on the bed with Kent and let him rub my hair till he fell asleep. Again, I discovered it was the simple, ordinary things I missed.

One Saturday in particular stands out in my mind. It was one of those days when I really felt like shit! I was in the kitchen, which was a disaster from Don making one of his famous Saturday morning breakfasts, and I was desperate to figure out what to do to make it through the day. My three men, Don, Kent, and Casey, were following me around.

"What are we going to do today?" the boys begged.

"What should I do with the kids?" Don inquired. They all needed me, and I just couldn't get myself together. Don ended up taking the boys to the pool, and they all came back exhausted, with colds, mismatched clothes, and bathing suits that were too big on them. My poor boys! They needed me!! And I was again reminded things just did not run smoothly without Mom around! Dad was amazing but exhausted from doing it all on his own; the boys were whiny and grumpy; and I was ready to have my life back. The life that I so easily took for granted was now so full of meaning.

My mom would take care of me during the day. She did our grocery shopping, cooked dinners, and took the afternoon shift with the boys. I missed having the energy to race Kent in the backyard in the after-noons. Casey wanted to try to ride his bike with the training wheels off, but I didn't have the energy to run alongside him and teach him how to balance and ride. I missed all of Kent's T-ball practices. In order to make it to a game, I had to plan on staying home and sleeping all day just to have the energy to make it through one of his games at night. One event, that's it! I was forced to realize a very cruel reality. My days, even my good ones, had boiled down to planning for one single event each day. Anything more and I was wiped out.

These last four months have forced me to slow down dramatically. At least for now, I cannot go from six a.m. to 11 p.m. anymore. But, being forced to slow down helped me learn to appreciate lying on the couch with Kent and watching TV, taking a nap with Casey, playing checkers, reading *Spider-Man* or *Winnie the Pooh*. There were many sacrifices. We did not go out to dinner, run from party to play groups, or even go to school functions, at least not as a family. Instead, we hung out together at home and just spent low-key time together. I know now that it is this time that is the special time.

These days, I have the energy to get up and make the boys breakfast and lunch, and Don can leisurely get ready for work. EVERYONE is hap-pier. What I know now is that being a mother is the most important job that I could ever have. As Don's father so eloquently described for me in an e-mail one day when I was bitching about not working, "You have a very important job. You are responsible for three young men that would be lost without you." His words of wisdom meant so much to me then and are so true to me now! My boys were lost without me. I am the spiritual leader of my home. I am the provider of peace, comfort, and love. These are gifts I feel NO ONE but a mother can provide. I am experiencing LIFE. I now know that it is the ordinary things in life that are extraordinary.

Given the opportunities I have been graced with, women today can have it all. We just cannot have it all at the same time. Thank God I took the time to experience Casey as a baby and experience being a mother full-time. You never know when it will all be taken away. Due to breast cancer and my treatment, I cannot have more children. Because this choice was taken from me, now, more than ever, I want to experience having a baby for one last time. So, I feel the need to shout loudly that having children is a gift from God. We should all relish in the experience of being pregnant, giving birth, and raising our children. We should also respect and love being a wife and developing and growing a marriage. This in itself is a full-time job that provides the foundation for loving, empathetic, confident children who will, in turn, grow into loving, empathetic, and confident adults.

What I know now is that no one can replace me in my role as a mother. Certainly, my positions at Procter & Gamble and Johnson & Johnson were easily filled. However, my job with my husband and my children is irreplaceable. This is where my heart and soul are fulfilled. Now I know that my work as a mother is, and always will be, the most important and fulfilling thing I will ever do.

I get it now.

PART III

LESSONS LEARNED

CHAPTER 9

MY TOP TEN LIST

Along with the stories these unsung heroes of everyday life shared with me—this last year taught me a variety of things about being a stay-at-home mom. The lessons seem too numerous to mention, but here are my top ten highlights:

∾ #1 I Am Not Alone ∾

How reassuring to know that I am not alone! The wide range of emotions that I have been experiencing, the ones that range from elation to frustration, are not, as I thought, symptoms of a bipolar disorder but, instead, are symptoms of being a stay-at-home mom. After reading what these bright, loving, and successful women had to share about their transition from "Corporate America" to "Carpool America," I feel validated. I feel a kinship with these women. I feel that I am not the only mom who is grappling with how to redefine themselves in this new backdrop, filled with burping cloths, endless grocery lists, and Play-Doh sculptures.

For the last year, I've been baffled by my conflicting thoughts. Part of me was so happy to have the time to spend with my kids so that I didn't miss their fleeting youth. The other part of me didn't feel complete. I felt guilty for having days where I thought I was going to pull my hair out. I felt inept for having thoughts like, "Maybe I am not cut out to be a stay-at-home mom!"

After reflecting on what this job called motherhood entails, I now believe that it is my God-given right to have days where there is doubt. In what other profession are people satisfied with their jobs 24 hours a day, seven days a week? I have women friends who are career women who complain about office politics. Others who have gripes about the grueling hours they have to put in. Still more confide that deadlines and/or employees are causing them undue stress. Ours is the only job where griping or complaining once in a while is not socially acceptable.

We were raised watching shows like "Leave It to Beaver" and "The Brady Bunch" that presented a warped view about being a stay-at-home. Unlike June Cleaver, making dinner for my family and greeting my husband with his slippers and pipe are not the highlight of my day. Unlike Carol Brady, I do not have an unwavering smile plastered to my face, even when my kids are breaking an antique heirloom. You never heard these media-created housewives vent about the demands that are placed on a mom. Our society has created an unrealistic expectation that mothers are not allowed to have "bad days." Everyone is entitled to have some bad days mixed in with the good. If they don't, they are either in denial or have a large supply of Valium.

Why is it that these employed friends of mine are given all the latitude in the world to bitch and complain about the strife they encounter in the business world, but stay-at-home moms don't have the same concessions? Maybe it's the fact that if we share our thoughts, we will be viewed as unfit mothers. Maybe, like me, they envision HRS waiting by the sidelines to snatch our children if we voice even the slightest dissatisfaction about the role we have chosen. Maybe we are simply being too hard on ourselves. We are human, and the state of being human means we are feeling creatures, blessed with a variety of emotions. If we did not experience pain or grief, we would, conversely, not be aware of our feelings of joy and happiness. I love being a mom, and my children are fantastic. That does not mean, however, that my job as a mom is without its challenges. The tide is beginning to turn, because women are starting to talk about the challenges, as well as the rewards.

∿ #2 Clean Your Emotional House ∿

This isn't the traditional broom and mop type of cleaning house to which I am referring. I am talking about cleaning up your "emotional house." We dedicate such a large portion of our lives attending to physical messes. We are constantly bending down to pick up dirty socks that have been strewn across the living room floor; scrubbing the grout between the tiles where a year's worth of mold has accumulated; or wiping muddy handprints from the hallway walls.

But, how often do we tidy up in our personal lives? When you make any life change, a shift occurs. People who once identified with you in a certain role (whether it be "boss," "colleague," or "breadwinner") no longer have that frame of reference. Once you remove yourself from the backdrop of the office, people may be at a loss as to how to identify with your newly chosen role as stay-at-home mom. This is extremely normal. It's like taking a buffalo from its herd and dropping it in the midst of a flock of flamingos. The buffalos don't understand why you left them, and the flamingos are trying to figure out why you have horns and don't stand on one leg. What happens during this transition from working full-time outside of the home and working full-time as a mom is that you initially get caught in this chasm. At the onset, you are neither a buffalo nor a flamingo.

The trick is to find true friends who understand your desire for change and who will support you in this pursuit. You need to rid yourself of false friends who try to sabotage your efforts with unsupportive comments. You'll recognize them as such because they will take on some variation of the following "well-intentioned" remarks:

"Boy, I don't know *how* you do it. If I had to stay home all day, I'd blow my brains out!"

"Don't you miss all the money you made?"

Or, my personal favorite, "How do you fill up your day now that you don't have a *real* job?"

The types of people who ask these questions are not your allies. They are undermining your decision to be a stay-at-home mom. This is when it becomes imperative that you surround yourself with positive, like-minded people who want the best for you.

Your setting has changed and so must your infrastructure to meet your new needs. That's when you get out your figurative vacuum cleaner and suck out all the negative influences that are polluting your life. You hang on to those old acquaintances and friends who are adapting with you and are offering support and encouragement. At the same time, you will be spending time in the new backdrop of motherhood where you will meet other stay-at-home moms who understand some of your current challenges.

When you are creating a new role for yourself, it is vital to keep friends and family by your side who want to see you succeed. If you remove the "clutter" from your emotional life, you will be greeted with a clean path on which to start your journey.

∾ #3 Laughter Is Better than Prozac ∾

Somewhere between the lipstick drawings on the walls and pennies shoved into the slot of our VCR/DVD player, I waved a big white flag. "I surrender!" I proclaimed to myself. I am the classic control freak who likes everything "just so," and I have come to the realization that this is simply not possible when you have kids.

Kids are spontaneous; kids are creative; kids have a knack for turning seemingly innocent, everyday household items, like a feather duster, into "weapons of mass destruction." I did the same things as a child. At age five, I was curious to see if the toilet would dispose of bigger objects, like clothing. I took off my charming, two-piece, pink polka-dot bikini and flushed it, just minutes before we were leaving for a day at Lake Michigan. There was also the time, at age nine, I remember giving my brother a home haircut (read: scalping) on the night before his organ recital. Needless to say, he had to sit facing a certain direction so that the "good side" of his head was facing the audience. I did my fair share of things when I was little that made the veins in my dad's head bulge out. I was no angel.

As a parent, however, I had conveniently erased all the silly and stupid things that I did as a child from my memory banks. I had a perverse expectation that my kids would grow up without incident. Don't ask me where this model came from, because I am very aware that other areas of life do not always unfold in a smooth and orderly fashion. So, I finally realized that I had a choice. I could either: a) choose to be so angry and upset that I was certain to have a heart attack or a stroke before the age of 50 or b) laugh at the situation.

I chose door number two. Between stress and laughter, I must say, laughter wins, hands down. Once I put the things my kids do, which would ordinarily cause a sane person to unravel, into the context of "that is just part of being a kid," I gave myself a very big gift. Firstly, there is less furrowing of my brows. The reward for me is that the frequency of my headaches has decreased and possibly the fact that I won't have to resort to Botox injections any time soon. Secondly, I stopped yelling as much. The reward here is obvious: I don't scare my children (and my husband) by turning into an unrecognizable, ranting woman. This tolerance has made me more approachable. I can only reason that if they can see that I am accepting of them, then they will be accepting of themselves and of others. They will look at the *full* package—the good along with the bad. After all, that's what unconditional love is, isn't it?

Lastly, by using humor to deal with the situation at hand, I realize that I can't control what has already happened. What's done is done. But, I do have control over how I choose to react to the situation. This was a major breakthrough for me. After years of trying to keep a tight grip on the reins so that I could give myself the sense that I was steering a situation in the direction I chose for it to go, I loosened the reins so that I could enjoy the ride without strangling the "horses" or without giving myself calluses from holding on too tight. This is not to say that I have fully abandoned getting stressed out by hospital visits or that I don't worry needlessly about red Kool-Aid being spilled on my off-white carpet. It just happens less often.

Some people think that humor is an inappropriate way to deal with life's little upsets. I'd say to these people that they haven't paid attention to their bodies the last time they had a good laugh. Your body tingles; your eyes dance; your cheeks hurt from laughing, but in a good way. Others join in. How often does someone "join in" when you are yelling? Not too frequently. When you are laughing, it is communal. By trying to recognize the humor in a situation, it has made my life more enjoyable.

∽ #4 Accepting Help Doesn't Make Me Any Less Wonderful ∽

From the time that I was old enough to string together sentences, "I can do it by myself" became one of my favorites. Call it independence or call it stubbornness—I wanted to show anyone around that I had what it took to do things *on my own*. It didn't matter whether it was getting myself dressed or putting a puzzle together; I didn't want people to help me. I'd look at something with dogged determination and stay glued to the task at hand until I had completed it. Much to my parents' dismay, this was not a phase that I grew out of.

I wore my independence like a badge of honor, with my chest puffed out and chin held high. I remember when I was graduating from college. Sorority sisters and other friends would discuss interviews that had been arranged for them by friends of their parents.

"Are you kidding me?" I scoffed. "Why go to college if you're going to have to rely on Mommy and Daddy to find you a job?" I reasoned. This wasn't sour grapes, either. My family had a handful of networking contacts ripe for the picking, but I would have nothing to do with it. The trend continued into the early part of my career. I preferred to work on projects by myself. I didn't want to rely on someone else's knowledge or expertise because I wanted to be self-reliant. So, there I was, toiling away, by myself.

Although this need for independence persisted, I did soften a bit in the later years. I formed a business partnership with a colleague, Mike, while I was at Merrill Lynch. I was now sharing tasks and forming goals alongside someone else that would affect my career. I credit Mike for taking me kicking and screaming from my outdated, isolationist ways of thinking into a fresh and unique perspective called "teamwork."

I noticed several shifts immediately. Egos were put aside. There was no longer room for my "me, me, me" or "mine, mine, mine" routine. Yet, alas, when I gave this up, magical things began to unfold. Our business practice took off. Our business was growing exponentially. We complemented each other perfectly. My skills and strengths coupled with his skills and strengths made the perfect union. (It was like a great marriage but without the sex.) By utilizing each other as sounding boards, we were able to refine our ideas and attract clients that neither of us would have been able to attract on our own.

Then, as my heart was calling me in a different direction professionally, my brother Mike became my partner. He agreed to join me in creating a children's charity, The Golden Rule Foundation. To this day, he claims that I would have started it on my own. (This is what happens when someone grows up watching you being fiercely independent; they begin to think that you really don't need their help.) This couldn't be further from the truth. He underestimates the encouragement and inspiration that he provides for me. Knowing that Michael "had my back" and shared my vision to create the foundation gave me the courage to move forward with this very big undertaking. Without accepting his help, the foundation would have been just another one of those "great ideas" that stay on paper and never materialize.

It wasn't until I became a stay-at-home mom, however, that I realized how much I had grown. There were parts of staying home that were very scary to a recovering independence-aholic. Not making my own money was at the top of the list. If I didn't earn my own paycheck, then I would be reliant on Brad for my livelihood. He welcomed the opportunity to become sole breadwinner, but for me, I perceived this as a form of being indebted to him. Would I have to ask for an allowance? Would I have to ask for permission to make purchases? Would I be forced to use oral sex as a type of commodity that I could barter and trade with him? (If the last was the case, I might really become broke!) I felt my independence melting away, quicker than ice cubes on a hot Florida day. "Having no money of my own is fine. The fact that I'll be home with Jess and Zach will make it palpable," I repeated to myself a couple hundred times a day. Like most fear, it was "<u>F</u>alse <u>E</u>vidence <u>A</u>ppearing <u>R</u>eal." I had worried needlessly. You see, to me, I gave up my independence, but, in reality, I had finally become interdependent.

For the first time in our marriage, I began to notice all the things that Brad had provided for me besides a paycheck. For the past 22 years, Brad has always given me emotional support. Brad has stood by my side, unfaltering, no matter what I decided to pursue. The decision, itself, to become a stay-at-home mom is the best example. Brad supported my desire to be home with the kids, but it wasn't without hesitation. We had built a certain dynamic in our marriage, and that dynamic had always defined me as being a fairly large monetary contributor. Even in light of this, Brad was up for redefining our roles. We shifted, we juggled, we worked it out...together. Being able to become a stay-at-home mom was a dream that I would not be living if it were not for the selfless support of my husband.

∼ #5 No Matter How Busy You Think You Are, There Is Always Time to Give ∼

As nice as it is to accept help, it is doubly pleasant to extend it. Offering help to others is a win/win situation. You get to fill a need that someone else is desperately seeking, while simultaneously getting the payoff of feeling valued as a human being. Sure, on a daily basis, I was offering help to my children, but I wanted to broaden my scope. Volunteering my time has always been important to me, but it became essential now that I was not working. Whether you volunteer for an organized group, such as PTA or a local charity, or simply volunteer your time helping a neighbor or a friend, it is an exceptional way to deepen your sense of community. The length of time that you dedicate does not matter. Whether you give one hour or several months is a moot point. The act of looking outside yourself is, ironically, what lets you learn more about your character.

Most moms say that they want to "instill a sense of empathy and compassion in my kids," yet what we don't often realize is that children learn more by deeds than words. If they watch you volunteer your time, they are more likely to have that become a priority for themselves. Better yet, if they help you make brownies for a bedridden neighbor or come with you to serve a meal at a homeless shelter, then they internalize the importance of giving by *doing* versus seeing. I learned that I am a powerful role model for my children. By volunteering to help others in need, I can instill the notion of living a lifestyle where you are constantly treating others the way you would like to be treated.

∼ #6 There Is an "I" in Family ∼

As a new stay-at-home mom, I initially felt that since this was now my chosen profession, every minute of my day had to be dedicated to my family. My house should sparkle; my laundry shouldn't pile up; my refrigerator should be fully stocked; and a sumptuous dinner should be ready and waiting for my husband and kids when they arrived home. The only problem with this scenario was there was no time left for me. There were days when I needed a "Mommy Time-Out." Unlike time-outs we give to our children for misbehaving, this time-out was for *good* behavior—a self-imposed reward of sorts. It was essential to recapture time that was solely for me. Friends, who went back to a career after being at home full-time with their kids, joked that they returned to work just so they could have a five-minute coffee break to themselves.

I didn't want to grow resentful that I no longer had a life to call my own. My adult time-outs included a mixture of relaxation and pampering. I used to feel guilty when I splurged on a pedicure or treated myself to a massage. It wasn't that I didn't feel worthy; it was that it felt too egocentric. Now I realize that these things are not selfish. These things are "investment spending" for the well-being of my family. When I allow myself to relax, it recharges my spirit.

I found the balance that I was so desperately seeking all these years. How can you be a good caregiver if you never take good care of yourself? If you spend all your energy on others and never focus on your needs, then eventually, there won't be anything left to give. No, I didn't need a big Swedish masseur named Günter to help me relax. Sometimes, I took walks. Other times, I took a bath. (We have a beautiful Jacuzzi in our bathroom that has managed to stay untouched for the last six years!) By taking these much needed breaks from my daily routine, I was able to rid myself of stress and found that it enabled me to give more of myself to others.

In addition to relaxing, I found it was equally crucial for me to find hobbies. My brain was screaming for something to keep it stimulated. Learning to fly became my passion. Having something that I always wanted to do and finally having the chance to pursue it was extremely empowering. It bolstered my self-esteem. It gave me a new way to define myself. I was no longer Rachel the Businesswoman; I was Rachel the Pilot! It also gave me something to talk about at cocktail parties besides what fabric softener worked best.

I now make a conscious effort to live outside my comfort zone by doing something that has been on my "always wanted to try this" list. Sure, it scares me a little, yet it helps me see myself from a different angle. For me, stretching my inner boundaries is as much of an adrenaline rush as closing a big deal. I decided to take advantage of the time during the day when Zach and Jess are in school to look at this chapter of my life as a learning opportunity. By trying on this new role as stay-at-home mom, it not only has brought me closer to my kids, it has afforded me the chance to discover and fulfill my dreams—dreams that always seemed so far off but are now at my fingertips. Finding my passion has helped me to find myself.

∽ #7 Enjoy the Moment ∽

I literally built a career on planning for the future. Save money for college, save money for retirement, take this job as a stepping stone so that one day you'll be qualified for the next job. Everything was a means to an end. I had been ignoring the here and now. I'm a rational person, so I am not advocating ditching all common sense about laying out action steps for what life may bring. What I have found, however, is that if you are constantly looking two weeks ahead or two years ahead, you are not enjoying the moment. Similarly, if you are always looking at past decisions and regretting choices you have made, then there, too, you are missing the here and now. It's like trying to drive your car while looking in the rearview mirror. You don't know what is going on right in front of you if you are focused on what is behind you.

For the most part, I wanted to consider myself present and "in the moment" while I was working outside the home. Yet, when I was honest with myself, there were plenty of times where I was guilty of being physically in one place when my mind was far, far away. There were times when Jessica would be telling me about a movie she saw, and I was bobbing my head up and down like one of those toy Chihuahuas people place on their car dashboards; but in reality, I was trying to figure out how I was going to fine-tune an upcoming presentation. Other times, when I would be playing cards with Zachary, instead of letting his infectious giggles wash over me, I was mentally going down my list of things that needed to get done before the weekend. I justified this behavior by saying I was practicing "good time management."

Little did I know that by justifying my actions, I was only cheating myself. I wasn't getting more done. Instead, I was becoming undone. My conversations became superficial; my gestures of kindness became almost robotic. I was just going through the motions. Choosing to go through the motions robbed me of having emotions. Once I made the switch to being a stay-at-home mom, I had the luxury of a bit more time. With this precious commodity, I was able to slow my pace. To a certain extent, I was able to curtail my planning so that I was doing more living in the moment. I started to use all of my senses. I became aware of not just what words spilled from my family's lips but noticed the body language that accompanied them. I would take notice of the smell of shampoo on Jessica's freshly showered head. I would marvel at how soft Zach's skin felt as I rubbed lotion on his back. I rediscovered the special gleam in Brad's bright, blue eyes.

I felt like a person who had just been given a second chance at life. This was my opportunity to make sure that I didn't let the present slip through my hands. Most people who have a brush with death will tell you that they experience this type of awakening. I consider myself extremely lucky that, in my case, all it took was a major life change. Do I still glaze over on occasion when I have to watch a puppet show for the 14th time in two days? Absolutely. The difference is, however, that I am aware that I am glazing over. Now, when this happens, I am able to catch myself in the act. I remind myself of how lucky I am to have children and a loving husband. I remind myself of how lucky I am to have another day to share with the ones I cherish. I remind myself that it is only two more hours until their bedtime!

∼ #8 "Having It All" Does Not Necessarily Mean Having It All at Once ∼

I had spent decades trying to live up to a preconceived notion about what it is to be an accomplished woman. All the bra-burning women that came before made great strides with the women's movement. The women who fought for equal opportunity opened doors that, without their persistence, would have remained slammed shut. Women were released from their shackles of domestic servitude, and, in record numbers, former housewives and daughters of former housewives claimed their rightful place in corporate America.

Women knew they had something to prove. "I can do anything a man can do...maybe better!" was the theme song of this generation. It was the mantra we said to ourselves when we woke up in the morning. It was the proverbial beacon of light at the end of the tunnel when we were trying to claw our way to the top. The women who were pioneers in the women's lib movement certainly gave us the opportunity to make our mark in the business world.

The only downside to having the "keys to the kingdom" was that some of the women, who were now on the fast track to the top, still had a maternal instinct gnawing at them inside. These women still wanted to fulfill their dream of having a family and raising children, complete with the white picket fence.

So, here sat the dilemma. Which path did we take? We were at a fork in the road. "Do I pursue a career, or do I start a family?" we pondered. "Do I bolster my self-esteem and claim my independence by earning a salary of my own, or do I become a mom?" we fretted. On the one hand, money and respect are good things. On the other hand, raising another human being is pretty special, too. Which to choose? Chocolate or vanilla? Peanut or plain? Salt or pepper? I'm not sure if the answer was born out of the same Gloria Steinem attitude of "You can have it all!" but there it was. Be both. Take both. Be everything at once.

The great juggling act began. Women chose to take on multiple roles. Negotiate mergers during the day and negotiate your way through your lasagna recipe for dinner. We were the breadwinners while simultaneously being the moms. We were kicking butt and taking names during the daylight hours, and we were wiping butts and noses at twilight. Having it all! Ah, yes, having it all...having high stress, having headaches, having no personal time whatsoever, having divorces, having affairs, having guilt. Guilt is a biggie. We were damned if we do and damned if we don't. When we went off to work and dropped our children at daycare, we were feeling guilty for abandoning them. If we took sick days off to tend to our children when they were ill, we felt guilty that we left our clients hanging. It seemed we had created an un-winnable game. Not only did we endure our own guilt feelings, we had guilt flung at us like bad cafeteria food from mothers who chose not to work.

"How can you leave your kids with strangers?" they would ask incredulously.

"How can you let yourself be dependent on a man for income and shelter?" we working moms would counter.

Guilt. Guilt. And more guilt. There had to be a way to deal with the pressures of "having it all" without self-destructing—without sacrificing our families or our careers and without crushing our spirit in the process.

Like all obvious answers, there was the solution staring me in the face. The women's libbers did have it right. We can have it all. However, nobody said we had to have it all *at once*. It sounds like such a small and subtle distinction, but, to me, it was a huge revelation. I can have a career. I can have a family. Who mandated that it needed to be simultaneous? Today's stay-at-home mom is a "new breed" of stay-at-home moms because she has the power of choice.

∼ #9 We All Have the Power to Choose ∼

Unlike our mothers and grandmothers, we were given the opportunity to demonstrate that, in the business arena, we are a force to be reckoned with. We redefined the roles that women are capable of playing. No longer are we cast as laborers on a manufacturing line. We own the manufacturing plant. We are doctors, lawyers, politicians, engineers, astronauts, and CEOs. We have shown that we have the desire and the drive to accomplish anything we want.

This is tremendously empowering because now, when we choose to be stay-at-home moms, we can do so with no remorse. We aren't plagued with unanswered questions about our ability to stand on our own two feet. When we choose to be stay-at-home moms, we have nothing to prove. We have climbed the ladder of success and realized that the view from the top just wasn't what we had in mind. We know that there is more than one way to feel like you are on top of the world, and it needn't be a view from a ladder. Conversely, women have the choice to return to the workforce after they have had children. They know what is best for themselves, and they are making a choice that will bring them the most pleasure or help them to achieve their personal goals. There is no "right" decision. It is not a "one size fits all" proposition. Each of us gets to ask ourselves, "Which scenario is right for me?" More importantly, each of us gets to determine if *both* scenarios are right for us. If they are both important to us, we then can decide if the two choices should be made in tandem or if one should precede the other. Nobody ever said that we had to eat the chocolate *with* the vanilla. If you like both flavors, eat vanilla today, and eat chocolate next week. Nobody should be dictating that we eat a swirled cone! The technology age, however, has made the choice of having both at the same time be more attainable. There are millions of women who are deciding that they want both a family and a career, simultaneously. The caveat being, they want it with less stress. Home businesses are springing up all over to provide women with yet another life choice. Building a career from home allows us to avoid long commutes; allows us to set a flexible schedule; and creates a balance between both worlds of career and family. Just remember, you make all the choices. You are the author of how your story unfolds.

∼ #10 There Is Only One Title of Which I Am Truly Proud ∼

I used to be all about titles. What position could I get where the name-plate in front of my corner office would dazzle and impress? When I graduated from college, I began the quest for the perfect executive position. The years went by, and as they did, I acquired a variety of different titles. There was "Project Coordinator," "Field Marketing Manager," "Assistant Vice President," "Co-Founder," and "Executive Director." I deluded myself into thinking that a loftier, more important sounding title and position would make me feel whole; that somehow, my value as a person would appreciate in direct proportion to the amount of money I was making or the number of people I was managing.

I couldn't have been more off base. The titles came, but the empty feeling remained. Don't get me wrong; there was the momentary elation that I experienced when the positions were initially secured, but it lasted about as long as the joy one gets when they find that unbelievable pair of designer heels on sale. In other words, the feeling was fleeting. Yes, there were *aspects* about the positions I held where I felt accomplishment and pride. There were programs I created, problems I solved, and people I helped. The payoff, however, did not meet my expectations. There were pats on the back; there were "thank yous" bestowed; there were even occasional celebrations for milestones reached. Why, then, did I not feel fulfilled?

It wasn't until I tried on the new title of "Stay-at-Home Mom" that the pendulum began to swing in the other direction. At first, I felt embarrassed to wear the title. "That's *all* you do?" I could hear others judging me, in my mind. I was afraid of how other people would size me up with no title to refer to for clues about my competence. I was so concerned about other peoples' perceptions that I lost sight of the only person that mattered—me. *I* had decided to change my priorities. My decision to stay at home was so that I could dedicate my time and myself to my children. No longer did I have to miss family dinners due to client meetings that ran late. I was now able to attend school plays; help throw class parties; chaperone field trips; and be an active participant in my kids' lives.

The truth was, even though I mourned the loss of my career, I liked who I saw staring back at me in the mirror each day when I woke up. What do I have to show for my new title? No paycheck and no fancy office; no awards and no staff; no couture wardrobe or lavish trips. Yet, I do have healthy and happy kids—kids who are grateful to have me close by when they need someone to turn to for advice or simply want to play; kids who tell me daily that they love me. Kids who know that they are important and that they are loved.

I now know how much I am valued. Giving life to another human being is miraculous; being able to shape a human being's life is priceless. I am now aware of how powerful a title I am holding. Nothing parallels the pride I feel wearing the title of "Mom."

∼ Diary Entry 117 ∼

The school year has started, and I have a lot of mixed emotions. Jessica is actually a freshman in high school! The thought that our already boy-crazed daughter is mingling with sophomore, junior, and senior boys with raging hormones doesn't exactly thrill me. She made captain of her cheerleading squad, so her confidence is growing, while the material on her skirts seems to be shrinking! I won't obsess too much, though, because I am sure that she'll continue to make smart choices.

Zachary started first grade at a new school and loves it. I like it, too, except for being deluged with the newest Sally Foster fund-raising drive. I swear, I *just* got rid of the closet full of wrapping paper left over from Jessica's elementary school years. (The chocolates we purchased went much more quickly.) Zach wanted to try a different sport this season and is now trying his hand (I mean foot) at soccer. Has it come down to this? I am now an official soccer mom? Well, I refuse to get a van with soccer balls emblazed on the back end. Maybe I'll opt for an unconventional soccer tattoo on *my* rear end? Well, I'll have time to decide. After all, I now realize that the decision is mine. Any decision is mine and mine alone. It does not matter what role I'm in. I can be at the helm of a company, chairing a black-tie gala, or raising my children, and I have the freedom to choose the path I take on any given day. I am in the driver's seat. The only thing that may hold me back is my own internal dialogue and self-imposed boundaries, which are disappearing with each day that I spend as a stay-at-home mom.

I wouldn't change the last year for anything. I have shed the cloak of guilt that I used to wear for thinking that I was not offering my best to my kids. In its place, I have wrapped myself in acceptance, and it feels warm and comforting, like swaddling myself in a towel that has just been heated in the dryer.

Becoming a stay-at-home mom has been the most liberating experience of my life. I've learned more about myself in the last 365 days than I have in the preceding four decades. The power to create a life that I love is amazing. Being with Jessica and Zachary is truly a gift. By looking at life through my children's eyes, it has reconnected me with my inner light. I have started to get the answers to life's most mysterious question: "What am I here for, and why was I created?" I am giving love and receiving love. I have created life. Now, I am creating lasting memories. Well, it's time for me to fly...both literally and figuratively!

ABOUT THE STAY-AT-HOME MOM CONTRIBUTORS

Ieshia Ali

A former Telecom operations manager for France Telecom, NA, Ieshia now enjoys being with her 15-month-old baby Yasin. She found a special way of dealing with the hectic pace of motherhood through her hobby as a yoga instructor. Ieshia's advice to aspiring stay-at-home moms is "Collect, assemble, and accept the help and kindness of friends, family, and strangers. Support is crucial to your sanity and success!"

Mary Susan Buhner

Before staying home to raise her children, Susannah (5½)and Caroline (3) and Baby (due in 2006), Mary Susan Buhner had a successful and rewarding career in the not-for-profit sector. With a degree in speech communication from Indiana University and a management certificate in fund-raising from the well-respected Center on Philanthropy, she led fund-raising efforts for several educational institutions. As executive director of the Lawrence Township Foundation, she worked with The Lilly Endowment to raise $1 million for the public school system. As an endowment campaign director for Indiana University, she helped configure and implement a national feasibility study for the university's $350 million Endowment Campaign. She was also responsible for securing major gifts for Butler University and the YWCA. Raised in the South, she now resides in Fishers, Indiana with her husband Zach. She serves the greater Indianapolis community through organizations like the Junior

League of Indianapolis, St. Luke's United Methodist Church, United Christmas Service, and Indiana University's Alumni Club.

Joy J. Bunville

Joy is a full-time mom, first and foremost, in her current journey of life. She has been married for nine years, and prior to their new family dynamic, she began her career as a teacher's assistant and then became a social worker, helping with wards of the state in Illinois and Ohio. It was after the years of assisting children that Joy knew she had to do what made her heart leap: She began acting and writing. Joy is a Screen Actors Guild member. She has worked on several filming projects and the stage. She has published small pieces of work, and her daughter, Samantha Noel, is in the entertainment business alongside her mom. Joy graduated from Loyola University of Chicago with a BA in English and philosophy. While pushing herself to fulfill her creative goals, she has taken the LSAT and considers law school in the future.

Lora Crone

Lora, a native Floridian, grew up in Dallas and now lives in Maitland, Florida. She earned her Bachelor of Journalism from the University of Texas, and following college, she started her own public relations, merchandising, and special events firm. In the early '90s, she accepted a position as sales manager for a sporting goods manufacturer and remained there until she and her husband decided it was time to stop traveling and create some little Crones—of which there are now two. Although Lora is a stay-at-home mom, she is a partner with her husband in their real estate development and custom home-building company. When she is not carting a child around or at a school volunteering, she can be found on the tennis court or planning a party.

Gina DiPaolo

Prior to becoming a stay-at-home mom, Gina was a financial analyst. Now a gratified mother of two children, Christian, age seven, and Ava, age four, she fills her days creating special moments with her kids.

Gina enjoys reading, cooking, gardening, and staying fit. To those women contemplating the decision to become a SAHM, she says, "Do it! The most interesting people you will ever meet are our own children."

Ann-Marie Dombrowski

A former administrative assistant to the director of NTC Events and supervisor of US Open Graphics Department, Ann-Marie is now a mother of four-year-old Ashley Marie. In between managing her household, she finds time for her new competitive sport—shopping. She admits she also makes time for finger painting and drawing on the driveway with chalk. "When I first became a stay-at-home mom, I felt very alone; nobody really understood the changes I was going through. Because of this, I felt compelled to tell my story to prevent other stay-at-home moms from feeling alone and misunderstood."

Camie Dunbar

Camie graduated from Florida State University with an undergraduate degree in media communications/business. She has 15 years in the marketing arena, where she has created successful marketing programs for companies such as Clear Channel, Perfumania, and Ofra Cosmetics. Currently, she oversees Dominate Marketing Group, Inc. and is the proud mother of 2½ -year-old Madison, with another on the way. In her spare time, she is a board director for The Jim Moran Youth Automotive Training Center, and she assists with fund-raising programs for Here's Help.

Christi Bowler Elflein

Christi was born and raised in Jacksonville Beach, Florida. She holds a Master's of City Planning from the Georgia Institute of Technology and a Bachelor of Science in social sciences from Florida State University. As a city planner, she has lived and worked in such cities as Atlanta, Georgia; Vail, Colorado; Fort Myers, Florida; and Orlando, Florida. In October 2000, she married Bill Elflein, and today they have a son, Jack. After five years of practice for other community planning firms, she is now president of her own planning consulting business, nuVisions, LLC, and lives in Norfolk, Virginia. She received the Georgia Planning Association's Planning Document of the Year Award in 2000 for her work on the Cheshire Bridge Road Corridor Study. Christi is a founding member and regional director of the Congress for New Urbanism Orlando Chapter, a board member of the Congress for New Urbanism Florida Chapter, active in the Downtown Orlando Partnership, and a member of the American Planning Association.

Leslie Fleischman

Leslie Fleischman, born and raised in New York, is an avid reader and writer. She currently resides in Scotch Plains, New Jersey with her husband Larry and is thrilled and fulfilled being a stay-at-home mom to her three children and their pup. This is the first of many stories that will come from her heart.

Queta Gavin

Queta, a former administrative assistant, left the workforce due to a bout with leukemia—a fight that she is winning. She is an active and involved mother in the lives of her two grown girls, Yolanda and Quiana. Queta utilizes her outgoing personality to volunteer her time with current leukemia patients. When she is not raising money or raising spirits, she can be found with the other members of the Red Hat Society, Motown Chapter, which she established.

Deidre Groehnert

Deidre was born and raised in northern New Jersey and graduated from college in 2000 with a BA in psychology, including two study sessions abroad. After graduation, she worked for 13 years in international trade for Bogen Photo, Hitachi, GE, and Sony. Positions included import/export law specialist, project management, certified black belt, and manager of Six Sigma Program. In 1997, she married Steve, a pharmaceutical scientist who was strong and kind and stole her heart. In 2003, they had their first child, Thomas James, which inspired Deidre to find a path toward at-home work. She is currently a happy mom to Tommy, writing and working in advertising out of a home office while pregnant with twins who are due in 2006. Deidre has always loved children, photography, writing, travel, and family celebrations.

Jennifer Hamman

A former therapist, Jennifer is the mother of two kids, Kyle, age 15, and Grace, age three. When she is not running her little one to the park or the beach, Jennifer runs her home-based business, RmdEagle Corp. Between naps and play dates, Jennifer enjoys reading. She suggests that women who want to become stay-at-home moms should "look at all areas of life, including finance, personality, and activity level. Talk with your spouse about everything, because it does change the dynamics of how you think and live."

Christine Louise Hohlbaum

Christine Louise is the official SAHM expert for ClubMom, award-winning American writer and author of *Diary of a Mother: Parenting Stories and Other Stuff* (2003), *SAHM I Am: Tales of a Stay-at-Home Mom in Europe* (2005), and has been published in hundreds of publications. She has a BA from Smith College in political science and German literature. From the University of Constance, Germany, she obtained her combined Master's degree in international relations/German and English literature. She has appeared on numerous programs, including NPR's The Parent's Journal with Bobbi Conner, Defining Women, ApPARENTly, Star-Style, WorldTalkRadio, WAHM Talk Radio, and the Mom Radio Network. She has appeared in *The Boston Globe Magazine, Pregnancy* magazine, *Ladies' Home Journal, Parents,* and *Woman's Day.* She teaches two online courses: "The Journaling Parent" and "How to Market Your Book." In addition, she is a motivational speaker. When she isn't writing, leading seminars, or wiping up messes, she prefers to frolic in the Bavarian countryside with her husband and two children. She invites readers to visit her Web site at www.DiaryofaMother.com.

Donna Maria Coles Johnson

Donna, a former attorney, has an entrepreneurial spirit that she follows while being a loving wife and mother of her two children, Vanessa and Brooks. She has started such businesses as The Lifestyle CEO Media Corp, LifestyleCEO.com, and the Handmade Beauty Network, HandmadeBeauty.com. The US Small Business Administration, Washington, DC, named Donna Maria 2003 Home-Based Business Advocate of The Year. Her advice to stay-at-home moms is simple. "Don't try to live up to any external standards. Live your life the way you and your family need it to be lived."

Donna Jones

Donna is an award-winning writer and public relations professional. Her articles have appeared in local, state, and national publications. Her work in the field of entertainment publicity and PR has spanned the country, raising awareness for education funding needs, environmental concerns, and promoting family entertainment. Donna currently works on editorial projects from her home in Altamonte Springs, Florida, which she lovingly shares with her husband Brian and their son, Hunter.

Theresa Joyce

This former property manager is now a mother of three children. She utilizes her time management experience to try to do housework while simultaneously entertaining her brood. When she's not attending extracurricular activities for her children, she enjoys photography, singing, and baking.

Brenda Jurbala

Brenda was born in Kittanning, Pennsylvania in 1965. In 1987, she graduated from Temple University with a BS in physical therapy. After working in various facilities as a physical therapist, she later became director of physical therapy at Aliquippa Hospital and then served as director of rehab in two long-term care facilities. She married her husband Rich in 1991 and had their first child in 1993. Being unable to conceive more biological children, she adopted their first daughter, Katie, in 2001. In 2003, Brenda moved from Pennsylvania to Florida, and later, in 2003, she adopted their second daughter, Rebecca. Both of her girls were born in China. Brenda shares, "All of my children have been such blessings. It has been very rewarding being home with them. I would not change that decision."

Elizabeth La Pietra DeWoody

A former sales and marketing manager for consumer goods giants Procter & Gamble and Johnson & Johnson, Elizabeth now focuses her time and talents on her two boys. In addition to being social coordinator for her active family, she volunteers her time to cancer-related causes such as serving on the Susan G. Komen Board of Directors. Elizabeth's journey to stay-at-home mom has made her realize that "We shouldn't take the simple things in life for granted. They truly are the most precious that life has to offer."

Liz Lippoff

Liz Rabiner Lippoff began her professional career as a junior high English and journalism teacher, exposing young minds to Shakespeare plays, the three-part essay, and how-to-turn-an-assignment-in-on-time. When she and her husband David began to move every few years for his career, she became a most-of-the-time mom, raising two wonderful girls and volunteering on the side. What she found was a way to help others...and a new career when she was ready to get back to the business world. Now a freelance consultant, Liz has served as public relations director for a runaway shelter and interim public relations director for a local American Red Cross chapter. She has a growing list of business clients, particularly medical providers, who rely on her company, Liz, ink, for ongoing consultation or ad hoc projects, and she continues to work with a variety of non-profits on public relations and marketing issues.

Holly May

A former registered nurse and now a mother of four children, Holly masterfully juggles the demands of parenting with fitting in time for herself. She is an avid reader, enjoys cooking, and has started playing golf. Her advice to women considering becoming stay-at-home moms is "Do it! Kids grow up so fast. You can always work later in life; kids will only be young once."

Melissa Rajsky

Melissa Rajsky started her advertising career at 19 in Allentown, Pennsylvania. She was promoted to her first executive position one year later. After five years of career life, Melissa realized that a job doesn't love you back and met her future husband, Miro. Together they moved to Florida. Five more years of career life, and Melissa decided to start her own business. After eight years of an advertising design business and two beautiful children, she became a full-time momma. When her youngest became preschool age, she longed for a new career (part-time) and combined her favorite hobbies of thrifting and fashion into a clothing design business called raw materials: www.rawmaterialsbymelissa.com. Since starting the business six months ago, she is enjoying tremendous success, proving the second time around is always better.

Julianne Rettig

Julianne is a dedicated mother of two children, Emily, five, and Robbie, three. She left a thriving career as a paralegal to focus on her family. Her children are her top priority, but she also owns her own company, Legal Outsourcing Services. To foster her creative side, she has also established a company called Tasteful Totes (www.tastefultotes.net). Her advice to women who are new stay-at-home moms is "You must truly believe that your job is important, because if you do not believe it, no one else will. Ignore others' commentary and innuendo on why you are home. You (and your children) know why. That's what counts."

Lisa Spengler

Lisa Spengler has been a stay-at-home mom for the past ten years and has loved every minute of it! During this time, she has enjoyed working within the communities of Collierville and Franklin, Tennessee, by serving as a PTA board member, Brownie leader, preschool teacher, room parent, and church volunteer. Before life with children, Lisa grew up in Tampa, Florida and attended Florida State University. Upon graduation, she worked in the Governor's Scheduling Office in Florida and for Marketing Specialists Sales Company. Now that her youngest child has started kindergarten this year, Lisa will soon be reactivating her career path that she put on hold while her children were small. Lisa resides in Franklin, Tennessee with her two children, Allison and Andrew.

Carlyle Spina

Formerly a partner in Nature's Way Franchising Group, Inc., Carlyle is now a proud mother of twins, Kit and Van. She is a freelance writer and a marketing director for www.missmaggie.org, a free educational Web site promoting environmental awareness in kids kindergarten through sixth grade. When she is not running her household, she is running in races. She has successfully completed both the Marine Corp and the Disney marathons. For women thinking about making the transition to stay-at-home mom, she says, "It is not for everyone. It's not unusual to struggle making the commitment to stay at home full-time, because it is not easy. However, if you do make the choice, the rewards are huge!"

Lisa Starr

Lisa, age 36, has been married to Reggie Starr for ten wonderful years! She resigned from her full-time job as a research specialist to become a full-time at-home mom for her three sons in the summer of 2003. Reggie Starr is nine, Brandon Starr is six, and Justin Starr is three years old. Lisa grew up in Cherry Hill, New Jersey and graduated from Richard Stockton University. She currently resides in Virginia with her family. She enjoys cooking, swimming, scrapbooking, and bowling. Her passion is baking and making edible art. Lisa decided to continue her education five years ago and received her Master's degree in education from George Mason University. Lisa is the owner of The Little Star Art Studio. For more information, log onto www.ka-doodle.com. She teaches edible art classes for toddlers and preschoolers in Prince William County. She enjoys managing her role as mommy and entrepreneur. She is the PTO president at her sons' elementary school and the Advisory Council. In addition, Lisa is the play group/support group coordinator for the Woodbridge, Virginia Mocha Moms Chapter.

Michelle Stiles

Michelle Stiles is a twenty-seven-year-old Stay-At-Home mom to her three children, Haily, 4; Mackenzie, 3 and Savannah 1. She is raising her brood in Hanover, MI. Michelle shares that the best part of being at home with her kids is "being able to witness all of their 'firsts.'"

Lynne Ticknor

Lynne Ticknor, M.A., is a freelance writer specializing in parenting, child development, education, and behavioral issues. She has written for national publications, including *Parenting, Family Fun, Parents, Baby Years, The Christian Science Monitor,* and Bankrate.com, in addition to dozens of regional magazines, trade publications, Web sites, and newspapers. Her biweekly column, "Home Instead," appears on MommaSaid.net. In addition to writing, Lynne is a certified parent educator in Applied Adlerian Theory and independent consultant helping families on an individual basis. She has taught hundreds of parents strategies and techniques for building strong relationships. Lynne has an M.A. in counseling and personnel services and a B.S. in communications. She frequently speaks at schools, parenting groups, churches, and corporations. Lynne lives in the suburbs of Washington, DC with her husband and three children, ages eight, six, and three. Visit her Web site at www.lynneticknor.com.

Christine Velez-Botthof

Christine was born in Manhattan, New York. As a kid she loved to "act." She'd write and act out plays with her little brother for anyone who'd watch. This was later realized as an introduction to a dream—producing. It didn't come easy, though. In high school, Christine entered the banking industry, in foreign affairs, working as an intern. This led her to study business and foreign languages in college. Her background in finance led to a job on Morgan Stanley's trading floor in New York City, where she met her husband and partner in parenting. After several years in the banking industry, Christine made the switch to a field that would allow her to write—journalism. She's worked as a newsroom manager and field producer in cities like Orlando, Florida; Charlotte, North Carolina; and New York City. She's walked a thousand miles in a journalist's shoes, covering stories as far away as Cuba and as heart-wrenching as 9/11. It took the tragedy of the Twin Towers collapse to help Christine understand the value of family. And that's when she made the decision to get married and have a baby. And here she is, a stay-at-home mom, proud to be a part of this book. Christine is 35 years old and lives in Birmingham, Alabama with her husband Rick, her son, Chase Morgan, and their two dogs, BooBoo and Babs.

ABOUT RACHEL HAMMAN

She's not your ordinary soccer mom. She has been named one of the "Most Remarkable Women" on Barbara Walter's ABC show, "The View." Rachel has been featured in *Glamour* magazine for her philanthropic advances and has also been recognized for her ongoing community endeavors by being tapped as one of the "Eckerd 100 Outstanding National Volunteers." Armed with a B.S. degree in communications from Florida State University, she embarked on a career filled with a myriad of experiences. Rachel's initial position was as a program coordinator for the Muscular Dystrophy Association. It was here that her passion for helping others was cultivated. She then worked as a field marketing manager for consumer goods giant, E. & J. Gallo Winery. Rachel was in charge of recruiting, training, and marketing for five Gallo distributors in the state of Florida. From the world of wine, she moved to the financial services arena, where she was an assistant vice president with Merrill Lynch in the Private Client Group. She managed investment portfolios for corporations and affluent individuals with combined assets totaling more than $250,000,000 and helped her clients successfully reach their financial goals. While achieving a burgeoning bank account, Rachel felt something was missing in her life. Recognizing the profound impact her non-profit experience had provided and lessons it had taught her, she co-founded The Golden Rule Foundation, a children's charity dedicated to inspiring children to give to others. She spearheaded a movement that provided elementary school children with hands-on community service projects so they could realize the pivotal role they are capable of playing in our society. She spent the next five years at the helm of The Golden Rule Foundation as the executive director.

It is Rachel's current position, however, that is her most challenging and provides her with the bulk of her "material." She is a happily married stay-at-home mom with two beautiful children. Her dreams for the future are to keep others around her laughing and to have her children grow into motivated, competent adults who require as little therapy as possible.

WHAT MAKES YOU A FEARLESS, FABULOUS, WOMAN AFTER FORTY?

What have you ventured out to accomplish after reaching the age of forty that you wouldn't have dreamed of doing in the previous decades? (Did you learn a new language? Move to a different country? Win a battle with weight? Start a new business? Adopt children from overseas? Switch careers to a radically different field? Write a movie? Compete nationally in a sport?) What are your secrets for being braver and trying new things in this phase of your life?

Write a two- to three-page story sharing both your achievements and your advice and you might find yourself in the pages of my upcoming book, *Fearless after Forty!* It will become a must read for women who are rapidly approaching the big 4-0!

Visit www.RachelHamman.com for more details!

BOOK CLUB DISCUSSION QUESTIONS

1. How has the role of stay-at-home mom changed over the last several decades?
2. What are the common misconceptions about stay-at-home moms that those who work outside the home need to understand?
3. Are there any social stigmas that exist when you are a stay-at-home mom?
4. What are the things that these former executives miss most about their previous positions now that they have become stay-at-home moms?
5. What changes occur during the course of being home with children that keep these women gratified enough to remain outside the traditional workforce?
6. Has the role of husbands changed as these women have exited the workforce?
7. Are today's stay-at-home moms more empowered? How so?
8. What will the impact be on the next generation of children by having their mothers working from home vs. working outside the home?
9. Has being a stay-at-home mom opened up some avenues for women that they ordinarily would not have pursued if they were working full time outside the home?
10. How have these women found a balance between being a stay-at-home mom and not losing their own identity?